MICHAEL ASPEL'S SUPER

A Star

D0511084

1976 is a year when virtuall[...] getting the most out of the little money available. This book is designed to provide new and old but always exciting ways to make the food budget work to the consumer's best advantage.

Capital Radio's highly successful SUPER SAVER programme has already convinced thousands to get out of the habit of buying 'convenience' foods and concentrate on certain basic rules which when followed will cut the budget and provide the consumer with a rich and varied menu. This book contains the radio recipes plus basic ideas about cheap, quick and easy-to-prepare foods. For the programme's fans and those unlucky enough to be outside the Capital Radio catchment area, *Michael Aspel's Super Saver Cook Book* is an investment that will save you pounds . . . on your food bill that is!

MICHAEL ASPEL'S
SUPER SAVER
COOK BOOK

Penelope Nightingale

A STAR BOOK

published by

W. H. ALLEN

A Star Book
Published in 1976
by W. H. Allen & Co. Ltd.
A Howard & Wyndham Company
44 Hill Street, London W1X 8LB

Copyright © Capital Radio 1976

Printed in Great Britain by
Richard Clay (The Chaucer Press) Ltd, Bungay, Suffolk

ISBN 0 352 39883 3

FOREWORD

Penelope Nightingale is a human hob. She bubbles and raises temperatures and generates enthusiasm. She also happens to look appetizing, and has an instinctive understanding of how to present a menu that looks good, tastes good, and by golly, doesn't cost too much either.

Each week, Penelope bounces into the studios of Capital Radio in London, listens intently to our Supersavers feature, which reports on what's the best value in the shops that day, and then she selects the items for her Supersavers Recipe. Phone calls and letters subsequently flood in from listeners who want to confirm the number of tablespoonfuls or who want a neatly typed copy of the menu for their collection.

I know nothing about food in its raw state: I can't cook (except, perhaps, a muscular omelette) but I know people who can, and I regularly take home Penelope's Supersavers Recipes, present them to the expert, and sit back, knife and fork in hand, napkin tucked under my chin, waiting for the plates of steaming goodies.

Familiar or surprising, simple or exotic, the Nightingale menus have one – no – two things in common. They're delicious, and they're not expensive. If you don't agree, I'll eat my words.

Michael Aspel

CONTENTS

GENERAL INTRODUCTION

Even though I now cook for my living, as a career I started doing so comparatively recently, because after trying my hand at many different things I realized cooking was the thing I liked doing best and I've never been one for spending my time in a job I didn't like. I have always been fascinated by food and everything connected with it; I love eating, of course, and my greatest pleasure is sharing food with my friends and family. I enjoy working out what I'm going to cook, shopping is a pleasure for me and I don't even mind the washing-up. This great enjoyment of food is something which has stood me in good stead in many ways over the years and particularly when I've really had to watch every penny I spent; getting the best out of too little money has frequently been very necessary and something which became a kind of game for me. Under those circumstances knowing current food prices is vital, so when Capital Radio started giving a daily run-down on 'Supersavers' on the Michael Aspel Show, I was delighted. Many of the items mentioned each day were things I'd come to know and appreciate as a way for me to enjoy my food cheaply and still be able to share it with my friends. After some weeks of listening to Joan Shenton and then Sue Cook talking each morning about conger eel, squid, herrings and the cheaper cuts of meat, it occurred to me that many of the people might be very interested in taking advantage of the low prices of such things, but because we've got so much into the habit of buying expensive 'convenience' foods, might not know how to cook them. With this in mind I wrote to the producer of the show and suggested that it might be a good idea to combine the 'Supersaver' feature with some recipes on cheap food – in particular recipes for dishes that could be prepared quickly and easily by even the busiest housewives, or anyone doing the cooking for that matter.

David Lucas, for that is the producer's name, agreed that such an idea would probably be of interest to many people; so together we worked out how I should present the recipes on the radio, because telling other people how to cook something was quite new to me. At the time of writing this, I've done quite a number of radio recipes and it seemed time to put them together, add some more, mix in some basic ideas about cheap, quick and easy-to-prepare eating and make a book. Which is what we've done.

The fact that I am now a professional cook may scare some people off a little. It is a natural reaction for someone to say: 'Oh well, it's okay for HER. She probably has a big kitchen, lots of equipment and plenty of time to prepare things.' As a matter of fact, that is not the case. I'm a working girl, so my time for home cooking is severely limited. My kitchen is the average size kitchen found in most flats and I don't have space for lots of lovely equipment, however much I might want it. Anyway, most of the recipes and ideas were worked out long before I started cooking for a living so I was in exactly the same situation as any other person who has a busy life and has to be budget conscious. Obviously my work has helped me to enlarge on my home cooking; but to anyone reading and using this book I do want to make it clear that nothing outside a normal kitchen and no extra time is necessary to follow any of the recipes I give in the whole book.

Having said that I should explain that it is necessary to use quite a lot of forethought and planning, but that can save a great deal of time and effort, particularly when it comes to shopping; and if one has to shop with young children around that can make a great difference to life! I discovered very quickly that planning my menus for a week in advance was vital if I was to use my money to the best advantage. I found sitting down once a week to prepare my lists of meals and the shopping I was going to do very enjoyable. It gave me a chance to take advantage of special offers and bargains I'd previously seen promoted in shops and supermarkets and to really make use of recipes I'd cut out from papers and magazines and had left in a nasty mess in a drawer.

Planning also means being able to make the best use of left-overs. For instance, knowing that I was going to cook a chicken on Sunday meant knowing that what was left could be turned into either a risotto, because there was a special offer on rice that week, or savoury stuffed pancakes in cheese sauce because eggs and cheese were down in price. I also discovered that I could make many of my own baby-foods by sieving or mashing some of our adult food which was an enormous saving on expensive tinned products. Planning also helped me to be able to include in my budget suppers or week-end lunches for my friends. For special meals it is nice to be able to spend a little more money on the individual items, but there were many times when I couldn't afford to do that and my love of simple food was very useful. One of my favourite meals has always been an omelette, salad and cheese or fruit and that is still the format for many of my supper parties. I still happily serve great bowls of soup with hot french bread, cheese and fruit or an inexpensive pudding to my friends and no one has ever stopped coming to supper because of it. One close friend of mine, and he's a marvellous cook, has given me a meal of grilled herrings with mustard sauce and mixed green salad more than once and I remember those meals with great pleasure.

So here are a few 'basic rules' I made for myself in planning my meals and shopping on a weekly basis.

1 Whenever passing supermarkets, the butcher, etc., I take particular note of special offers, lower prices, etc., so that I can incorporate them into my next week's food.
2 I never buy anything just because it is cheap, unless it is something I use regularly and can be put in my store cupboard.
3 I always work out in advance how much I need of any item and I don't buy more than that, even when the person behind the counter wants me to!

4 I very rarely buy tinned or frozen foods if I can buy the same item fresh. And I never buy them unless I am satisfied that they are the best value I can get.

These rules are something which I'm sure everyone has worked out for themselves, but the important thing is to stick to them!

The next important thing I discovered about preparing cheaper food was that many dishes can be varied in content very satisfactorily. Of course in many recipes there are ingredients which cannot be changed, neither should the proportions be changed, especially if one is making a cake or pastry, etc. But more often than not there are times when a dish can be made far more cheaply by juggling with its contents a little. For instance, to quote chicken risotto again (and risottos are one of my favourites for making a tasty, filling and cheap dish from very little), the list of ingredients may well be: rice, stock, chicken, onions, mushrooms, tomatoes and perhaps peas. If mushrooms are expensive, leave them out; it's not necessary to buy peas for just one dish, so if you haven't any left over from a previous meal, substitute something else.

Maybe you have an odd sausage or slice of bacon in the fridge? Put that in your risotto. Any raisins or sultanas in your store cupboard? Put in a few of those. Maybe there's a tiny bit of tomato purée left in the bottom of the tube – mix it in – the result will be delicious. In other words, use what you've got and don't buy expensive items just because the recipe says so.

I have included quite a number of recipes for soup in this book, but that is a prime example of where variations can be made to suit your pocket. I suppose the saying 'Variety is the spice of life' is what one should remember here.

Another important factor in the organization of cheaper food is the store cupboard. As I have already said, I don't buy cheap items unless they can usefully go into my store cupboard. Many of the items in my cupboard are things I can make myself far more cheaply than buying them and the freezer compartment in my fridge is a supplement to my store cupboard. Don't imagine that I do things like preserve my own anchovies – I certainly don't – but I do make my own breadcrumbs for frying; I do make my own pickles and chutneys, and if I've got time, jam and marmalade too: I do keep tinfoil containers of stock in the freezer compartment, as I do a little store of pancakes, which are easy to make and are extremely useful stand-bys. And I do prepare many of my own fats and drippings for frying. Consequently, further on in the book, there is a little section about items which really do not need to be bought ready-made.

I see no reason to be shy about asking shopkeepers for freebies or cheap items which he might otherwise throw away; it's amazing how kind and helpful people can be if you bat your eyelashes at them!

For instance, I always ask my grocer or butcher if he has a ham-bone going spare – it will cost a few pennies but is delicious for soup and the dog loves it when I've finished with it. Many shops sell grated cheese bits cheaply, which is perfect for sauces for cauliflower cheese, fish, macaroni, etc. More than once I've taken home free of charge a bagful of cauliflower leaves for supper instead of an expensive vegetable. At the fishmonger fishbones shouldn't cost anything and they are what are needed for lovely fish soups, fish pie, etc.

There are one or two items I always keep an eye open for or ask for if I don't see them displayed, one of which is bacon bits, which are frequently available from the supermarket, butcher or grocer. The lean parts are excellent for many recipes using bacon and the fat part, when melted down in the oven, makes lovely dripping for the breakfast fried bread. And I know many people who love it spread on a slice of bread with a little salt. I do for one. Other items I snatch up when I can are bones and cheap bits from the butcher or supermarket. The bones make stock for soups and stews and the meaty bits can be minced for meat-burgers, spaghetti sauce and savoury stuffings for peppers, heart, and a great family dish, stuffed cabbage. I said earlier that extra time isn't really necessary for preparing cheaper food. To be truthful there is no doubt that to get the best from cheaper cuts of meat, they do need a little more time and care, but I know from experience that organization gives one the extra time needed. And, anyway, things like breadcrumbs and dripping virtually make themselves while you do something else.

I have also said that no special equipment is necessary to prepare my recipes, but there is one thing that is vital and that is a sharp knife. And I mean sharp. It is far easier and quicker to prepare food with a sharp knife than with a blunt one. Also you are less likely to cut yourself because you don't have to hack at things, which is how fingers usually get cut. I have two very special knives which go everywhere with me and are not for use by anyone else or for anything other than food. One is small for preparing vegetables and the other is a bigger one for everything else. If you are not able to sharpen your knife yourself, ask the butcher to do it for you, which he usually will if he's not too busy. If that is no good it is possible to buy a patent knife sharpener from the ironmonger.

I can hear people saying once again: It's all very well for HER, she likes cooking. So I do, but I know that many people don't and that some people actively dislike it. Well, that is a pity, because most people have to cook in some way or other. To those for whom the whole business is a beastly chore the only thing I can say is that I hope the sense of satisfaction gained from money stretching compensates a little. Perhaps you could buy yourself some roses from time to time with some of the money you save?

STORE
CUPBOARD

The following recipes are for things which most people will use from time to time. They are all easily prepared at home and are cheaper home-made than bought.

CHICKEN STOCK

Put any chicken bones, cooked or uncooked, and the giblets if you have them, into a large pot and cover them with cold water. Add a carrot, a small onion, a bay leaf, a piece of parsley, 6 black peppercorns and a celery stalk. Cover the pan and bring it to the boil. Skim off any froth which forms on top and add a cupful of cold water. Then let the stock simmer for as long as possible – until it has reduced by half and has a good strong flavour. To keep the stock, strain it and keep it in the fridge for about two days or freeze it.

BREADCRUMBS FOR FRYING

Breadcrumbs last a long time in an airtight jar and are easily made. Put slices of bread, preferably not too fresh, in a baking tin in a low oven. Allow them to become absolutely crisp and light golden coloured. Crush them with a rolling-pin, preferably between two sheets of greaseproof paper or foil, to prevent them going all over the kitchen floor! Store in a jar when they are absolutely cold.

DRIPPING

Frequently when you buy kidneys, they are sold with their suet left on – butchers will sell fat bits cheaply and bacon bits can also be bought cheaply. All can be turned into dripping. Cut the fat into chunks and leave it in a baking tin in a low oven to melt. Drain the fat off from time to time and store it in jars in the fridge. Each dripping will have a different flavour so keep them separate.

PANCAKES

It is worth spending a spare hour making a batch of pancakes – they can be used either with a savoury stuffing and cheese sauce, or for puddings, with sugar and lemon or melted jam. They should be kept in the freezer or freezer compartment of the fridge. Cook them in the normal way and allow them to cool on a sheet of greaseproof paper. Stack them one on top of the other, with squares of greaseproof paper in between each one and wrap them up into a parcel with some kitchen foil. To use, peel off as many as necessary, defrost them and if using them for a pudding reheat them in the oven, still with their papers between them, and wrapped in foil.

PANCAKE BATTER

$\frac{1}{2}$ pt. milk
4 oz. plain flour
1 egg
Extra egg yolk
1 dspn. oil
Pinch of salt

Sift the flour and salt into a mixing bowl and make a well in the middle. Into the well put the egg, the extra egg yolk, the oil and a spoonful of the milk. Gradually incorporating the flour, mix the eggs and flour to a smooth batter, adding the milk bit by bit. Before cooking allow to stand for at least half an hour. To cook the pancakes, strain the batter into a jug, adding a little more milk if it is too thick. Heat a small frying pan and grease it lightly with lard or oil. Pour into the pan just enough batter to cover the bottom thinly, cook it until golden brown, turn it with a spatula and cook the other side.

DRIED HERBS AND CHILLIES

Either tie up bunches of herbs and hang them in a warm dry place, such as the airing cupboard, or leave them to dry on a baking tin. When they are absolutely dry and crisp, crumble them up and store them in airtight jars or tins. Chillies, which are useful for curries, should be hung up to dry by threading a piece of cotton through their stalks. As they turn red while drying, they look quite nice hanging in the kitchen.

PICKLED ONIONS

2 lb. pickling onions
1½ pt. vinegar
2 oz. mixed pickling spice
4 tblspns. coarse salt

Peel the onions, lay them on a tray or shallow dish, sprinkle them with salt and leave for 24 hours. Boil the vinegar with the spices for about 5 minutes, then strain it and allow it to go cold. Drain all the salty liquid off the onions with a sieve or colander, and pack them into jars. Fill the jars with the cold spiced vinegar and cover the jars with waxed papers. Do not use metal lids. The pickles will be ready to eat after 5–6 weeks.

SWEET APPLE CHUTNEY

3 lb. apples, cored and chopped
2 lb. onions, chopped
½ lb. raisins
1 lb. dark brown sugar
1 tblspn. salt
½ pt. malt vinegar

Put everything into a casserole and cook the chutney until it is soft. Then mix it with a wooden spoon until it is pulpy and allow it to go cold. Put it into jars and cover with jam papers.

PICKLED RED CABBAGE

3–4 lb. red cabbage
1 pt. malt vinegar
2 oz. mixed pickling spice
½ lb. coarse salt

Peel away the limp outer leaves of the cabbage, cut it into quarters and slice it finely – discarding the thick white stalky bits. Spread the cabbage on a tray or shallow dish, cover it with the salt and leave for 24 hours. Shake off the liquid with a sieve or colander then pack the cabbage into jars. Meanwhile, boil the vinegar with the spices for about 5 minutes, strain it and allow it to go cold. Pour the vinegar over the cabbage, making sure there are no bubbles left in the jars, and cover the jars with jam papers. Leave for a couple of weeks before using.

FRESH TOMATO SAUCE

1½ lb. chopped tomatoes
½ lb. chopped onions
½ tspn. dried basil or 1 tspn. fresh basil
1 clove garlic, crushed
½ tspn. sugar
1 dspn. oil
1 wineglass cider
Salt and pepper

Fry the onions and garlic in the oil until soft and pale yellow. Add all the other ingredients and cook until the tomatoes are really soft. Put the whole lot through a sieve and keep in the fridge or freezer. This sauce is ideal for serving with fish, chicken, pasta, etc.

FRENCH DRESSING

French dressing is most easily made and kept in a screw-top jar and shaken before using. It is difficult to give precise proportions for making it because it depends on individual taste, however 3 parts of oil to 1 part of vinegar or lemon juice is a good starting-point. Add to that, salt, black pepper and a little sugar. A clove of garlic, a teaspoon of french mustard or half a teaspoon of mustard powder can all be added as well.

SARDINES WITH VINEGAR AND CREAM

1 tin sardines in oil
Salt and pepper
1 dspn. vinegar
1 tblspn. cream or top of the milk

Drain the sardines thoroughly of all the oil (don't throw it away, give it to the cat!). Split them and remove the bone and stringy fibres inside each one. Mash the prepared sardines in a bowl with the salt and pepper and approximately 1 dessertspoonful of vinegar to taste. Then mix in the cream and leave the sardines to cool in the fridge for an hour or so. Serve with hot toast and butter.

SARDINE PÂTÉ

For a small starter for 4 people I consider 1 tin of sardines to be quite enough but some people prefer to use more. For a very special meal I have substituted smoked salmon for the sardines; not, I should say, the expensive sliced variety but the offcuts which some fishmongers and delicatessens sell very cheaply. These bits take time to prepare but the result is worth it. Separate the fish from the skin and boney parts, put it through the mincer and proceed in the same way as for the sardines.

1 tin sardines in oil
Lemon juice to taste
Equal weight of butter
Salt and pepper

Drain the sardines very thoroughly, split them and remove the backbone and any stringy bits inside. Mash them in a bowl with a little salt and pepper and lemon juice to taste. Mix in an equal weight to the sardines of softened butter –

NOT melted butter – until the pâté is really smooth. Pack it into a little pot and leave it in the fridge for an hour or so to firm up. Serve with hot toast.

DEVILLED SARDINES

1 tin sardines
Salt and pepper
1 small slice fried bread per person
$\frac{1}{4}$ tspn. mustard powder
Dash of Worcester sauce

Drain the sardines thoroughly, keeping the oil for frying later. Split each fish and remove the backbone and any stringy fibres. Spread the fish on a plate and sprinkle them with the mustard, pepper, salt and a few drops of the sauce. Leave them for about half an hour then fry them in the oil from the tin. Serve hot on a small slice of fried bread.

MARINATED KIPPER FILLETS

Believe it or not, the flavour of this dish is in the luxury class; I suppose it could be called the poor man's smoked salmon. But it will only be like that if fresh kippers are used, not the fillets found in little plastic bags. (Of which I have a very poor opinion.) The best way to buy kippers is to choose the fat juicy ones but for a starter 1 whole kipper is too big for one person, so allow 2 kippers for 3 people. For the recipe below 3 kippers for 4 people is more than enough.

3 kippers
Juice of 3 lemons
1 large onion
Fresh black pepper

The kippers are not to be cooked, so with a sharp knife remove the head, tail and backbone, plus any other stray bones that you can. If you have time, skin the remaining fillets and cut them into 2-inch pieces. Slice the onion into very thin half rings. Place the kipper fillets and onion in alternate layers in a shallow dish, pour over the lemon juice and add a good sprinkling of black pepper. Keep the kippers in the fridge for as long as possible before serving, spooning the lemon juice over them as often as possible. The longer this dish can be left to marinate the better so it is best prepared on either the morning or evening before it is to be eaten. Serve it as it is, or with brown bread and butter.

PICKLED HERRINGS WITH APPLE AND MAYONNAISE

4–6 pieces pickled herrings per person
¼ eating apple per person
1 dspn. mayonnaise or salad cream per person

Drain the herrings thoroughly. Core and thinly slice the apple and leave it in a little water and lemon juice for a few minutes to prevent browning. Layer the fish and apple slices in a shallow serving dish, pour over the mayonnaise or salad cream and serve chilled.

CRISPY FRIED SOFT HERRING ROES

1 lb. soft herring roes
Seasoned flour
4 wedges of lemon
1 beaten egg
Crisp breadcrumbs for frying

Wash the roes gently and remove any fibres left on them. Poach them very carefully for 4–5 minutes until they are firm. Drain them and pat dry with a cloth. Roll them in the flour, then the egg and then the breadcrumbs. Fry in hot deep fat until golden and serve them hot with a wedge of lemon.

SOFT ROES WITH PARSLEY BUTTER

$\frac{3}{4}$ lb. soft herring roes
1 clove garlic
Salt and pepper
2 oz. butter
1 dspn. chopped fresh parsley
4 slices of toast

Wash the roes thoroughly, dry them and season them lightly with salt and pepper. Melt the butter in a frying pan, add the garlic clove sliced into thin pieces and the finely chopped parsley. Fry the roes in the butter until they are firm and cooked through – about 4–5 minutes. Remove the garlic from the pan, pile the roes on to the hot buttered toast and pour over them the hot parsley butter.

COD'S ROE FRITTERS

These are best made when you've been making pancakes because not very much batter is needed and it is a waste of time to make a batch of batter specially.

2 $\frac{1}{2}$-in. slices boiled cod's roe per person
Pancake batter
1 wedge of lemon per person

Dip the slices of roe in the batter and fry them in deep fat until golden. Serve with a wedge of lemon.

14

SCRAMBLED EGGS WITH TARRAGON

This dish is best made in the summer when fresh tarragon can be bought in little bunches in markets and good greengrocers. However, not having fresh tarragon should not stop anyone from preparing it; use the dried herb instead because the result is still very good.

4–5 eggs
1 oz. butter
Salt and pepper
4 slices hot buttered toast
1 tbspn. top of the milk
1 dspn. chopped fresh tarragon
Or:
1 tspn. dried tarragon

Mix all the ingredients together very thoroughly and make the scrambled eggs in the normal way. Please don't overcook the eggs – they really are best if served slightly creamy and not in the horrid hard little lumps presented by hotels, cafés and places that ought to know better.

STUFFED EGGS

4 hard-boiled eggs
1 tspn. chopped parsley
½ tin sardines prepared as for sardines with vinegar and cream
Lettuce leaves or sliced cucumber or tomato to garnish

Cut the eggs in half lengthways and carefully remove the yolks. Mash the yolks with the sardines then pile the mixture back into the egg halves. Sprinkle the finely chopped parsley over each egg and serve them with a garnish of lettuce leaves, sliced cucumber or tomato.

OEUFS EN COCOTTE

This is the grand French name for eggs baked in little oven-proof dishes, one per person. The eggs can be baked by themselves or with a bed of cooked spinach or fried onion and bacon. They are served straight from the oven with or without toast, but as toast fills people up a bit I always serve it!

1 egg per person
Salt and pepper
1 tspn. top of the milk or single cream per person
Optional extra:
**1 spoonful cooked drained spinach mixed with a
    little nutmeg**
Or:
1 spoonful chopped fried onion and bacon

Butter the little ovenproof dishes and if using one of the optional extras put that into the bottom of each dish. Break one egg into each dish, taking care not to break the yolk. Season with a little salt and pepper and pour on the cream. Place the dishes in a roasting tin and pour into the tin enough boiling water to come half-way up the side of the dishes. Bake in a fairly hot oven – Mark 5 (375°) – for 8–10 minutes. The egg whites should be firm like a soft-boiled egg so that the yolk is still soft in the middle. Serve immediately in the dishes.

CODDLED EGGS WITH FRESH HERBS

Coddled eggs sounds very motherly somehow! Really all it means is eggs that are boiled for 3–5 minutes, depending on their size, and then placed in cold water to cool. Having been cooked this way the eggs should be shelled very carefully so that they do not break, then gently sautéed in 2 ounces of butter in a frying pan, with a little salt, fresh black pepper, a squeeze of lemon juice and a large spoonful of either finely chopped parsley or chives. Serve them hot in their golden buttery sauce with plenty of fresh hot toast.

LEEKS VINAIGRETTE

This is one of my favourite starters; in fact I'm very fond of beginning a meal with vegetables in a vinaigrette dressing because they are very light and a pleasant way of whetting the appetite.

1 leek per person
Vinaigrette dressing
Salt and freshly ground black pepper

Wash the leeks thoroughly so that there is no grit in them and cut them into 1-inch rings. Either steam or boil the leek pieces in salted water until they are cooked through but still slightly crisp. Drain them very well indeed and while still hot pour over enough dressing to cover them well but not make them too soggy. Serve slightly chilled with freshly ground black pepper.

TOMATO AND ONION SALAD

1 tomato per person
1 small onion per person
1 tblspn. Vinaigrette dressing per person
Chopped fresh parsley to garnish

Slice the onions and tomatoes as thinly as possible. Place them in alternate layers in a shallow serving dish or on individual plates, pouring a little dressing over each layer. Serve slightly chilled with the chopped parsley sprinkled over.

CUCUMBER AND ONION RAITA

1 large carton of unsweetened natural yoghurt
½ cucumber
1 medium onion
Paprika

Wash and dry the cucumber and cut it into very tiny cubes. Chop the onion finely. Mix them both into the yoghurt and chill for at least an hour before serving. Serve with a sprinkling of paprika over the top. This is lovely on hot summer days and is also the perfect accompaniment to curry.

CELERY AND COTTAGE CHEESE WITH FRUIT

2 or 3 sticks of celery per person
8 oz. cottage cheese
Either:
1 finely chopped eating apple

Or:
Some chopped tinned pineapple
Or:
Some sultanas
Or:
Some chopped block dates
French dressing
Finely chopped fresh parsley

Scrub clean the celery and cut it into bite-sized pieces. Mix the cottage cheese with the chosen fruit, pile it into the celery and leave in the fridge for an hour or so to chill. Just before serving pour over a little french dressing and sprinkle on the parsley.

If using a chopped apple remember to leave it in some water with some lemon juice in to stop it going brown. The apple needs to be left in the water for only a couple of minutes, but not only will the apple not go brown, its flavour will be improved as well.

MUSHROOMS IN YOGHURT OR SOUR CREAM

This is nice when mushrooms are cheapest or have been picked in the country one day. If buying mushrooms, the tiny button ones look nicest, though the bigger open ones have a stronger flavour and should be sliced.

$\frac{1}{2}$ **lb. uncooked mushrooms**
2 tblspns. French dressing
1 tspn. chopped fresh parsley
1 small carton natural yoghurt
Or:
1 carton sour cream

Clean the mushrooms but do not peel them. Mix them in a bowl with the dressing and the parsley and keep turning them from time to time, until all the dressing is absorbed. 10–15 minutes before serving add the yoghurt or sour cream and chill in the fridge. Garnish with a little extra chopped parsley and serve with hot french bread.

ONION TART

This dish can be served both as a starter or as a main dish, hot or cold. The servings per person are smaller if it is to be served as a starter, which may leave some over for eating cold next day. Very economical!

6 oz. shortcrust pastry (6 oz. flour, 3 oz. butter
or marge and a little water to mix)
3 lb. sliced onions
1 oz. fat for frying
2 oz. grated cheese

Make the pastry, roll it out and line an 8-inch flan or dish with it. Bake it blind. That is, cover the pastry in the tin with greaseproof paper or foil, fill it up with rice or haricot beans and bake it in a good oven – Mark 6 (400°) – until it is a good golden colour. Remove the rice or beans and the foil and the pastry case is ready for use. Meanwhile cook the onions gently in a covered pan with the fat for about 30 minutes; they should be quite dark in colour but not at all crisp. Pack the onions firmly into the pastry case, cover with the grated cheese and return the flan to the oven. Bake it until the cheese has melted and become a golden brown topping.

N.B. – Don't throw away the beans or rice you used for baking the pastry case. When they are cool store them in a jar to use again.

ORANGE SALAD

4 medium oranges
2 tblspns. French dressing
1 dspn. chopped fresh mint
½ Spanish onion or 1 medium onion
1 dspn. chopped fresh parsley

Peel the oranges with a very sharp little knife, removing the pith at the same time. This is done by peeling around the orange just as one does when trying to take the peel off an apple in one long spiral. Cut the oranges into thin slices and the onion into very thin slices. Mix them together in a bowl with the fresh herbs and the dressing and leave in the fridge for an hour before serving.

GRAPEFRUIT AND BROWN SUGAR

½ grapefruit per person
1 dspn. demerara sugar per grapefruit half

Prepare the grapefruit in the normal way by separating the segments with a sharp knife. Cover each half with a dessert-spoon of brown sugar, packing it into a good firm layer. Put under the hottest possible grill for about 1½–2 minutes so that the sugar melts. (Do not test it with your finger or you will get a very nasty burn.) Allow the grapefruit to go cold and the sugar will solidify into a crisp golden topping.

POTTED CHICKEN

This is ideal for using up the left-overs from a roast chicken.

As much cold cooked chicken as possible
1 onion
1 tspn. chopped fresh parsley
Some melted butter
Salt and pepper
A little chicken or bacon fat for frying

Mince the chicken and mix it with the parsley. Chop the onion very finely and fry it till soft with the fat. Add the chicken to the onion and season to taste. If possible mix in some of the jelly left in the pan from when the chicken was roasted – if you did not use it to make the gravy, that is. Pack the chicken mixture into a suitable pot and when cold pour over some melted butter to cover. Allow the butter to set and then serve the chicken with toast; a little home-made sweet chutney served separately makes a delicious addition.

GARLIC BREAD

The scent of garlic bread is wonderful and really appetizing. The crispy outside of the loaf with its buttery garlicky inside is marvellous and an ideal accompaniment to soups and many starters.

1 small French loaf or 1 crispy roll per person
2 oz. butter
1 large or 2 small cloves of garlic
1 tspn. chopped fresh parsley (optional)

Crush the garlic and mash it into the butter with the parsley. Cut the loaf into slices or cut the rolls in half, without cutting through the bottom crust. Spread the butter on each side of the slices and put the bread into a hot oven for 5–6 minutes so that the outside is very crisp and the inside soaks up the melting butter. Scrumptious!

SOUPS

Soup is one of the budget-conscious woman's great stand-bys; not just because it is easy to make and can be made from just about anything, but because many soups can provide a filling and delicious and very cheap meal if they are eaten with fresh bread or hot toast with some cheese and fruit or pudding to follow. And soup really can be made from anything; vegetables, fish, meat and vegetables, with dumplings, meatballs, cheese or noodles. The possibilities are endless.

The following recipes are really ideas for soup, rather than sets ways of making it. If you don't have one of the ingredients available it doesn't matter; use more of what you have got or put in something else. There is one great basic requirement for soup, however, and that is good stock. Stock cubes are marvellous but obviously if you have made your own stock from the week-end's chicken carcase or meat bones, or from bones, etc., bought cheaply from the butcher, the soup you make will be that much cheaper and more nutritious. On the other hand, there is no reason why you shouldn't use your own stock *and* stock cubes.

CAULIFLOWER AND BACON SOUP

1 large cauliflower
½ lb. bacon bits, chopped
1 large onion chopped
2 medium old potatoes
1 clove garlic, crushed
Seasoning
1½ pt. chicken stock

Fry the bacon lightly in a casserole pot until the fat begins to run, then add the onion and garlic and cook them until soft and yellow. Cut the peeled potatoes and the cauliflower into chunks, using the cauliflower stalk but peeling the thick end piece, and add them to the pot with the stock. Bring the soup to the boil and simmer it until the vegetables are very soft. Season to taste. Either serve the soup as it is, or sieve or liquidize it. If doing the latter, some crispy fried onion or crispy fried bread croûtons make an ideal garnish.

CABBAGE AND FRANKFURTER OR SMOKED RING SAUSAGE SOUP

1 medium white cabbage
2 medium onions, chopped
1 clove garlic, crushed
1 small tin tomatoes
1–2 frankfurters per person
Or:
1 small smoked boiling ring
1½ pt. chicken stock
Salt and pepper
1 oz. fat for frying

Fry the onion and garlic in the fat until soft and yellow in a large casserole pot. Cut the cabbage into quarters then slice it thinly discarding the stalk. Add the cabbage and tomatoes to the pot with the stock and bring the soup to the boil. Cut the sausage ring into chunks, or if using frankfurters, leave them whole and add them to the pot. Simmer the soup gently until the cabbage is cooked. Season to taste and serve as it is.

POTATO AND CABBAGE SOUP WITH CHEESE

2 very large old potatoes
1 small white cabbage
1 large onion, chopped
1 clove garlic, crushed
1½ pt. stock
4 oz. bacon bits, chopped
Salt and pepper
2–3 oz. grated cheese

I seem to have said the first bit somewhere else sometime!
Fry the bacon bits gently in a big pot until the fat runs, then
add the onion and garlic and fry them until golden and soft.
Add the stock, bring the soup to the boil, then add the
potatoes, peeled and cut into 1-inch chunks. Simmer until
the potatoes are nearly cooked. Slice the cabbage very thinly
indeed, add it to the pot and boil the soup fast for a few
minutes so that the cabbage is cooked but not too soft and
the potatoes are completely cooked. Serve with the grated
cheese sprinkled over the top.

POTATO AND ONION OR LEEK SOUP

3 large onions
Or:
3 large leeks and 1 onion
3 medium old potatoes
1 clove garlic, crushed
1½ pt. chicken stock
1 oz. fat for frying
Salt and pepper
A little milk

27

Chop the onion and fry it with the garlic until soft and
yellow. If using leeks, clean and cut them into 1-inch rings
and add them and the potatoes, cut into chunks, to the pot
with the stock. Cook the stock until everything is very soft.
Either sieve the soup or liquidize it and return it to the pot.
Season it to taste and add enough milk to make the consistency you require. Serve with hot garlic bread.

BRUSSELS SPROUT SOUP

This soup is a delight to all lovers of sprouts, and good for
making when sprouts are at their cheapest, or a little ragged.

1–1½ lb. sprouts
1½ pt. stock
1 small onion, chopped
Some bacon bits, chopped
Salt and pepper
A little milk
1 tspn. fat for frying

Cook the sprouts in the usual way. Meanwhile, fry the onion
gently in a pot until it is soft and yellow. Drain the sprouts,
liquidize them with the onions and a little of the stock, or
put them through a sieve. Put the purée into the pan with
the stock, heat it gently, season to taste and add the milk
if necessary to get the consistency you want. Serve with the
bacon bits fried crisply and scattered on the top.

NETTLE SOUP

This is not as ridiculous as it sounds! Nettles taste like
spinach and are considerably cheaper. When gathering the
nettles take only the tender tops and do remember to wear

gloves . . . of course, once they are cooked nettles do *not* sting. Anyway here is the recipe for a soup of a quite spectacular green.

2 lb. young nettle tops
1½ pt. chicken stock
1 lb. old potatoes
1 clove garlic, crushed
1 large onion, chopped
Salt and pepper
1 oz. butter
A little milk

Fry the onion and garlic in the butter until soft and yellow. Meanwhile wash the nettles, put them into a saucepan, cover them with cold water and bring them to the boil. Strain them thoroughly and throw the water away. Add the nettles to the onions in the pot with the stock and potatoes, peeled and cut into chunks. Bring the soup gently to the boil and simmer it until the potatoes are cooked. Put the soup through a sieve or liquidize it, return it to the pot and gently reheat it. Season it to taste and add a little milk if necessary. Do cook this soup gently or the nettles will lose their colour and the soup will not be such a brilliant green.

GREEN PEA SOUP

1 lb. shelled peas
1½ pt. chicken stock
1 onion, chopped
1 clove garlic, crushed
1 sprig of mint
1 tspn. sugar
Salt and pepper
1 tspn. butter for frying
4 oz. bacon bits, chopped

29

Cook the peas with the mint, sugar and salt and then drain them, discarding the mint. Fry the onion and garlic in the butter until soft and yellow, add the bacon bits, fry for a few more minutes then add the peas and the stock. Bring the soup to boiling point and simmer it for 10–15 minutes. Put the soup through a sieve or liquidize it, reheat and season to taste. Serve garnished with tiny squares of fried bread.

BEETROOT SOUP

This is a recipe I stole from my favourite London wine bar, and is just about my favourite soup.

**1 lb. raw beetroot
1 large onion, chopped
2–3 sticks celery
2 carrots
1 clove garlic, crushed
¼ lb. bacon bits
1½–2 pt. chicken stock
Salt and pepper
1 dspn. sugar**

Put the diced bacon in a casserole pot or saucepan over a low heat and cook until the fat runs. Then add the onion and garlic and cook them until soft and yellow. Meanwhile, peel the beetroot and carrots and cut them and the celery into little matchsticks if you have time. If not, chop them. As the vegetables are prepared put them into the pot and give them a stir from time to time. Then add the stock and bring the soup to the boil. Simmer it for an hour or so, season to taste and, if necessary, add the sugar.

MINESTRONE SOUP

2 oz. tiny star noodles or finely broken spaghetti
1 large onion, chopped
1 large carrot, diced
1–2 sticks celery, cut into matchstick slices
1–2 oz. peas
1 clove garlic, crushed
1½ pt. beef stock
1 tblspn. tomato purée
Salt and pepper
A little fat for frying
Parmesan cheese

The vegetables for minestrone can be anything available – if using cabbage, slice it very thinly indeed. Fry the onion and garlic in a large pot until soft and yellow. Add the other vegetables, the stock and the tomato purée. Bring to boiling point, simmer very gently until the vegetables are practically cooked. Add the pasta, season to taste and cook for 10–15 minutes. Serve with the Parmesan or grated Cheddar cheese on top.

LENTIL SOUP

One of the best home-made soups in the world, filling and comforting on beastly cold wet days. If it is possible to buy a ham-bone cheaply from the butcher do so – otherwise any sort of bacon will do, as much or as little as you like, but at least 4 ounces.

½ lb. red lentils
1 large onion, chopped
1 large carrot, cut into rings
1 small tin tomatoes
Ham-bone or bacon

1½ pt. water or stock
Salt and pepper
1 oz. dripping
1 tspn. chopped parsley

Cook the onion in the fat until soft and yellow in a large pot, then add all the other ingredients, except the salt. (If using a piece of smoked boiling bacon, soak it overnight in cold water or the soup will be too salty.) Bring the soup to boiling point and simmer it until everything is soft – which should take approximately 1½–2 hours. If using a ham-bone or a piece of boiling bacon, remove it from the pot and chop the meat into dice. Return the bacon to the pot and season to taste. There are two ways of serving this soup – either liquidized or sieved or cooked until the lentils are so soft that they can be eaten as they are. The soup will be slightly 'chunkier' that way, but many people prefer it.

SPLIT PEA OR HARICOT BEAN SOUP

This is very similar to lentil soup – it can be cooked in exactly the same way, but the split peas or beans must be soaked in cold water overnight. Also the soup really should be put through a liquidizer or sieve.

FISH SOUP

This can be one of the cheapest soups to make because it can be made from what many fishmongers sell as 'cat pieces', i.e. cod flaps; that is, the thin piece of flesh cut from between the head and the top of the body. The only preparation needed before the fish is suitable for cooking is to separate the flesh from the bones, and that is not difficult with a sharp knife. Incidentally, cod flaps are ideal for fish cakes, crispy fish balls, fish pie, soufflé, flan, etc.

If they are being used for this soup, the bones make the necessary fish stock. If other fish is used, make the stock from fish bones which the fishmonger should supply free of charge. To make the stock, bring to the boil some sole bones, or fish trimmings, 1 bay leaf, 1 onion and some fresh parsley in 3 pints of water. Simmer the stock, after skimming off any froth which may form and adding a cupful of cold water, until the liquid is reduced by half, then strain it and it is ready to use. This soup can also be made with chicken stock, which, of course, makes the whole process of making it far quicker.

1½ pt. fish or chicken stock
Approx. 1 lb. white fish
1 large onion, chopped
1 leek, cut into rings
1 clove garlic, crushed
2 carrots, cut into rings
2–3 outside sticks of celery
1 dspn. chopped parsley
2 tblspns. tomato purée
1 large old potato, cut into chunks
1 oz. fat for frying

Fry the onion and garlic in a large pot until soft, then add all the vegetables, the stock, parsley and tomato purée. Bring the soup to the boil and simmer it until the vegetables are cooked. Ten minutes before serving, add the fish cut into bite-sized pieces, season to taste and continue simmering until the fish is cooked, but still in nice pieces.

FISH CHOWDER SOUP

This is another soup which is a meal in itself. It should really be made from one of the more expensive white fish, such as cod or hake, but I find that coley, whiting or red fillets are just as nice.

1 lb. white fish
2 thick slices belly pork (salted)
1 large onion, chopped
2 large carrots, cut into thick rings
1 large old potato
½ pt. water
1 pt. milk
Salt and pepper

Cut the rind off the pork and cut the meat into 1-inch squares. Fry them in a large pot until the fat runs, add the onion, and fry it until yellow and transparent. Meanwhile, poach the fish gently in the water with a little salt for 10–15 minutes. Remove the fish from the liquid and set it aside. Add the fish liquor to the pork and onions, also add the carrot and the milk. Bring the soup to the boil and simmer it until the carrots are half cooked. Then add the potato, cut into bite-sized pieces, and continue to cook the chowder until the carrot and potato are cooked. Add the fish, which has been flaked, skinned and boned, simmer for 2–3 minutes to heat the fish, season to taste and serve immediately.

CHICKEN SOUP WITH EGGS AND VEGETABLES

1½ pt. chicken stock
4 eggs
1 leek, cut into rings
1 onion, chopped
1 carrot, cut into rings
1 clove garlic, crushed

1 tspn. chopped parsley
4 slices bread
Fat for frying
Salt and pepper

The most important thing about this soup is really to have proper home-made stock with a good strong flavour.

Fry the onion and garlic in a large pot until soft and yellow; add the vegetables and stock and bring the soup to the boil, then simmer it until the carrots are cooked. Check the seasoning.

Break each egg separately into a cup then slide it carefully into the soup – poach the eggs for 4–5 minutes so that the whites are firm and the yolks still soft. Meanwhile, fry the slices of bread, put one in the bottom of each serving plate, place a poached egg on top and pour the soup over – serve with the parsley sprinkled over.

CHICKEN AND VEGETABLE SOUP

Like the previous recipe, home-made stock really should be used for this soup. This is marvellous for someone who hasn't been well and has no appetite.

1½ pt. good chicken stock
1 medium onion, chopped
1 clove garlic, crushed
1 large leek, cut into rings
1 large carrot, cut into rings
1 tspn. chopped parsley
1 tspn. chicken fat
4 oz. cooked chicken, cut into small pieces
Salt and pepper

Fry the onion and garlic in the fat until soft and golden yellow. Add all the other ingredients, except the chicken, bring the soup to the boil and simmer it until the carrot is cooked. Just before serving add the chicken pieces, season to taste and simmer the soup for a further 2–3 minutes.

PIG'S HEAD SOUP

Please do not be put off by the thought of using a pig's head – it really does make the most beautiful soup, in fact the sort of soup that is practically a meal in itself. Ask the butcher to prepare the head for you and cut it into large pieces.

$\frac{1}{2}$ **fresh pig's head**
1 clove garlic, crushed
1 large onion, chopped
1 leek, cut into rings
2 carrots, cut into rings
2 sticks celery, cut into pieces
1 bay leaf
1 tspn. chopped parsley
2 pt. stock
1 oz. dripping
Salt and pepper

Soften the onion and garlic in the dripping in a very large pot; then add the stock and meat pieces, bring it to the boil and simmer it for 1 hour. Then add all the other ingredients and continue cooking for another hour. By this time the vegetables should be cooked and the pork meat should come away from the bones easily. Remove the meat pieces from the soup, separate the meat from the bones, cut it into bite-sized pieces and return it to the pot. Season to taste. This soup is suitable for cooking the day before it is to be eaten and then gently re-heated. It is delicious served with thick slices of hot bread or toast and butter.

FISH
COURSES

HERRINGS IN OATMEAL
WITH MUSTARD SAUCE

1 herring per person, split and boned
Medium oatmeal or rolled porridge oats
2 oz. butter for frying
Salt and pepper

For the Sauce

1 tblspn. mustard powder
1 dspn. vinegar
1 dspn. sugar
1 dspn. top of the milk
1 oz. melted butter
1 tspn. chopped parsley

Clean the fish, leaving them damp so that the oatmeal will
coat them all over. Sprinkle the fish with salt and pepper,
and roll them in the oats. Fry them in the butter until crisp
and golden brown on each side. To make the sauce, mix
everything together.

PICKLED HERRINGS

This is a basic Danish recipe which can be varied by the
addition of mustard or horseradish, or by changing the pro-
portion of sugar to vinegar. If pickling this number of
herrings, they can be stored in sealed glass jars in the fridge.
Obviously, for 1 meal for 4 people, not so many herrings
are needed.

10 herrings, filleted
3 medium onions, thinly sliced
½ pt. white vinegar
6 oz. sugar
4 tspns. whole allspice
3 bay leaves
12 black peppercorns
½ pt. water

Cut the fish into 2-inch pieces then put them in a bowl in alternate layers with the onions. Put everything else into a saucepan and boil. When cool, pour the liquid over the fish and leave them to pickle for at least 12 hours in the fridge. To serve, drain the fish and remove the bay leaves and spices.

HERRING AND POTATO PIE

2 lb. filleted herrings
1½ lb. old potatoes, sliced into rings
2 large onions, finely sliced
2 eggs
¾ pt. milk
Salt and pepper

Butter a shallow baking dish and fill it with layers of fish, onions and potatoes, seasoning each layer with salt and pepper and finishing with a layer of potatoes. Mix the eggs into the milk and pour it over the pie. Bake it in a low oven – Mark 4 (325°) – for about 1 hour, until the potatoes are cooked through and the top is crisp and golden. Serve with tomato or mustard sauce.

BAKED HERRINGS WITH FENNEL

1 split and boned herring per person
2 oz. melted butter
Salt and pepper
1 sprig fennel per herring

Season the herrings inside and out, lay the fennel inside each fish and brush the inside with melted butter. Lay each fish on a piece of greased kitchen foil, fold the foil round the fish into a secure parcel and bake in a moderate oven for 20–30 minutes. Don't eat the fennel.

DEVILLED HERRINGS

4 herrings with their soft roes
1 tblspn. chutney
1 tspn. Worcester sauce
Vinegar
Salt and pepper

Have the fishmonger remove the heads from the fish and clean them. Soak the fish in vinegar for about 2 hours, with a teaspoon of salt. Mash the soft roes with the chutney and Worcester sauce and stuff the fish with the mixture. Season the fish with a little fresh ground black pepper then fry them in a little hot oil until the outsides are golden and crispy. This is a delicious dish served with creamy mashed potatoes.

GRILLED MACKEREL

1 mackerel per person
Parsley butter—finely chopped parsley mixed
    with butter and fresh ground black pepper
Approx. 1 oz. butter per fish

Have the fishmonger top, tail and clean the fish. Cut little diagonal slits on the sides of the fish, 2 per side will do, and pack the butter into the slits. Grill carefully, turning once, until the fish is thoroughly cooked and the skin nicely crisp. Spoon the juices over the fish as they cook and serve them with an extra squeeze of lemon.

GRILLED MACKEREL
WITH SOFT ROE STUFFING

4 mackerel, with their soft roes
1 egg yolk
1 dspn. finely chopped parsley
Finely grated peel from $\frac{1}{2}$ a lemon
Breadcrumbs made from 1 slice of bread
Salt and pepper
Butter for grilling

To make the stuffing – simmer the roes in salted water for approx. 10 minutes, then chop them finely and mix in the egg yolk, lemon peel, parsley and the breadcrumbs. Season the stuffing with salt and pepper. To cook the fish, fill them with the stuffing and grill them with dots of butter until they are crispy and golden.

MACKEREL WITH MUSHROOMS
AND FRIED TOMATOES

4 large mackerel fillets
1 onion, finely chopped
1 clove garlic, crushed
4 oz. mushrooms, sliced

1 tblspn. vinegar, preferably white wine vinegar
Seasoned flour
3 oz. butter

Roll the fish in the seasoned flour and fry them in 2 ounces of butter. Meanwhile fry the garlic, onion and mushrooms in the other ounce of butter. When the mixture is ready, add the vinegar, season it to taste and serve the fish with the sauce poured over and fried or grilled tomatoes handed separately.

BRIAN'S SPAGHETTI WITH TUNA FISH

This is one of my friend Brian Rich's store-cupboard stand-bys for unexpected guests – it's a recipe he brought back from an Italian holiday.

2 7-oz. tins tuna fish
1 tspn. chopped parsley
1 chicken cube dissolved in $\frac{1}{2}$ pt. water
1 garlic clove (optional)
Salt and pepper
1 pkt. spaghetti

Drain the oil from the fish and heat half of it in a frying pan with the crushed clove of garlic. Don't throw the rest of the oil away, give it to the cat! Add the tuna fish to the pan, breaking it up into nice-sized flakes. Add the chopped parsley then add the hot stock and simmer the mixture. Meanwhile, boil the spaghetti in salted water for approximately 10 minutes, then drain it thoroughly and serve it on separate plates with the sauce poured over. The nicest accompaniment to this is a crisp green salad with french dressing.

TUNA FISH SALAD

1 tin tuna fish
1 lb. cold cooked potatoes
2 hard-boiled eggs
1 onion
Chopped parsley
French dressing

Drain the tuna fish from its oil and flake it. Cut the potatoes
into thick slices and chop the onion finely. Combine all
three in a bowl and add enough dressing to thoroughly
moisten the potatoes, probably about $1\frac{1}{2}$–2 tablespoonfuls.
Allow to stand for half an hour, turning the mixture from
time to time. Just before serving, add the eggs, cut in half
and sprinkle with some chopped parsley.

FISH WITH CIDER SAUCE

This is a very useful recipe because it can be adapted for all
sorts of white fish, but if using conger eel, it will need baking
for $1\frac{1}{2}$–2 hours in the oven.

1 lb. chosen white fish fillets
2 onions
1 oz. butter
1 wineglass cider
$\frac{1}{2}$ wineglass water
$\frac{1}{2}$ oz. butter
1 oz. flour
Salt and pepper

Slice the onions and fry them gently in the $\frac{1}{2}$ ounce of butter.
When they are soft lay them on a greased fireproof dish and
lay the fish on top, sprinkling them with a little salt and

pepper. Heat the cider and water to boiling point, pour it over the fish, cover the dish and bake it for approximately 20 minutes at Mark 4 (350°). When the fish is cooked pour off the liquid to make the sauce and keep the fish warm. Melt the 1 ounce of butter in a saucepan, add the flour and cook it for 2–3 minutes, stirring all the time so that the flour doesn't burn. Remove the pan from the heat and gradually mix in the fish liquor, stirring to prevent lumps forming.

Return the pan to the heat, and bring the sauce gently to boiling point and allow it to bubble slowly for 3–4 minutes, stirring all the time. Pour the sauce over the fish and serve immediately.

ROCK SALMON WITH ONIONS AND TOMATOES

Like the preceding recipe, this one is also suitable for any type of white fish – coley, whiting, herrings, red fillets: all can be cooked this way.

1 lb. chosen fish, filleted
4 tomatoes or 1 small tin tomatoes
2 onions
1 clove garlic
1 oz. fat for frying
A little milk
Seasoned flour
Salt and pepper

Slice the onions, crush the garlic and fry them gently in the fat until they start to go golden. Add the tomatoes, peeled and chopped, and cook them with the onions for about 10 minutes. Meanwhile, cut the fish into 2-inch 'soldiers', dip them into the milk, then the seasoned flour and fry them in hot oil or fat until golden. Serve them with the onion and tomato sauce, which should be seasoned to taste.

WHITING IN CHEESE SAUCE

3–4 whitings, skinned and filleted
¾ pt. milk
1 oz. butter
1 oz. flour
4 oz. grated cheese
Salt and pepper

Lay the fish fillets in a greased fireproof dish and sprinkle them with salt and pepper. Melt the butter in a saucepan, add the flour and cook it for 2–3 minutes, stirring it so that it doesn't burn. Remove the pan from the heat, gradually mix in the milk, stirring to prevent lumps forming and add 3 ounces of cheese. Return the pan to the heat, bring the sauce gently to boiling point and allow it to bubble slowly for 3–4 minutes. Season it to taste. Pour the sauce over the fish, sprinkle the rest of the cheese over the top and bake in the oven – Mark 5 (375°) – for about half an hour, so that the fish is cooked and the cheese topping is bubbly and golden brown.

SKATE IN ORANGE SAUCE

1½–2 lb. skate
½ pt. milk
Salt and pepper

For the Sauce

Juice of 2 large oranges
1 onion
1 oz. butter
1 tspn. chopped parsley

5–6 drops of vinegar
1 tspn. sugar
Salt and pepper

Cut the skate into 2–3-inch strips and poach it very gently in the milk for 25–30 minutes. Drain it thoroughly and remove the skin. Lay the fish in a serving dish and keep it warm. Meanwhile, prepare the sauce by cooking the finely chopped onion in the butter until it is soft and yellow. Add the orange juice and all the other ingredients to the pan and bring them to the boil. Allow the sauce to bubble for a few minutes until the liquid has reduced a little and thickened, pour it over the skate and serve it immediately.

SKATE IN CHEESE SAUCE WITH ONIONS

1½–2 lb. skate
1 pt. milk
2 onions, sliced
4 oz. grated cheese
2 oz. butter
1 oz. flour
Salt and pepper

Poach the skate as in the previous recipe, then skin it. Meanwhile, fry the onions in 1 ounce of butter until they are golden. Into a greased fireproof dish lay half the onions, put the fish on top and cover it with the rest of the onions. Make the sauce by melting the other ounce of butter in a pan and add the flour, allow it to cook for 2–3 minutes, stirring it to prevent it burning. Remove the pan from the heat and gradually mix in the fresh milk, stirring it to prevent lumps forming. Return the pan to the heat, bring the sauce to the boil slowly and add 3 ounces of the cheese. Cook the sauce for 3–4 minutes, season it to taste, then pour it over the fish.

Sprinkle the rest of the cheese on the top and brown it under the grill until it is golden brown and bubbly.

FISH PASTY

½ lb. any cooked fish
1 hard-boiled egg
1 medium onion
1 tspn. chopped parsley
A little milk
Salt and pepper
1 oz. butter
1 small pkt. frozen pastry

Chop the onion finely and fry it gently in the butter. Chop the hard-boiled egg and flake the fish. Mix all these together with the parsley, seasoning and just enough milk to make the mixture moist. Roll the pastry into an oblong and lay the mixture along it. Fold the pastry over, moisten the edges so that they stick together. Brush the pastry with a little milk to glaze and bake the pasty on a greased baking tin, join side underneath, in an oven at Mark 7 (425°), or until the pastry is golden brown.

CRISPY FISH BALLS

1 lb. any chopped white fish
2 onions
2 slices bread
1 egg
1 tspn. chopped parsley
Salt and pepper
Fat for frying
Crispy breadcrumbs

Cut the peeled onions in quarters and boil them until soft in a little salted water. Drain them thoroughly, then chop them. Soak the slices of bread in a little water then squeeze them out. Mix the fish with the onion, bread, parsley, salt and pepper and enough beaten egg to bind. Roll the mixture into little balls, roll the balls in the crispy breadcrumbs and fry them until golden brown. Serve with tomato sauce.

FISH FLAN

This recipe was given to me by an American friend called Kate and is exactly as she wrote it, which accounts for all the 'cupfuls'.

1 pkt. short pastry
1 teacupful cooked, flaked fish (any kind will do)
1 large tomato
1 teacup sliced onion
$\frac{1}{2}$ teacup grated hard cheese
2 teacups milk
2 eggs, beaten
Salt and pepper

1. Roll out the pastry and line a flan tin.
2. Slice the tomato thinly.
3. Fill the flan with layers of onion, tomato and fish.
4. Mix the eggs and milk and season with salt and pepper. Pour this into the flan.
5. Sprinkle over the grated cheese.
6. Bake flan in a moderate oven until the custard is set and the top is nice and brown.

N.B. – Don't use expensive fish. The cheapest white fish makes a lovely flan. Serve hot or cold.

Note: I prefer to cook the onions until soft in a little butter, but it's really a matter of taste and how thinly the onions are sliced.

FISH SOUFFLÉ

½ lb. any cooked white or smoked fish
1 oz. butter
1 oz. flour
¼ pt. milk
4 eggs
2 oz. grated cheese
Salt and pepper

Mash the cooked fish thoroughly. Melt the butter in a saucepan, add the flour and cook it for 2–3 minutes, stirring to prevent it burning. Remove the pan from the heat and gradually mix in the milk, stirring to prevent lumps forming. Add the cheese and return the pan to the heat. Bring the sauce to the boil and let it bubble gently for 3–4 minutes, stirring all the time. Remove the pan from the heat, mix in the fish, then the egg yolks and season the mixture to taste. Whip the egg whites until stiff, then fold them into the fish mixture. Pour it into a greased 7-inch soufflé dish, or other high-sided dish, and bake it in a moderate oven – Mark 4 (350°) – for about 30 minutes, until the soufflé is well risen and golden brown on top.

TINNED SALMON PIE

1 tin salmon
1 large onion
1 hard-boiled egg
1 tspn. chopped parsley
1 tblspn. salad cream or mayonnaise
1 pkt. frozen pastry
Or:
Pastry made from 8 oz. flour, 4 oz. butter or
    marge and a little water to mix

Chop the onion very finely, chop the egg, drain the salmon (give the juice to the cat!) and mix them together with the parsley and salad cream. Divide the pastry in half and roll one half into a circle big enough to cover a 7-inch fireproof plate. Put the fish mixture in the middle, and moisten the edge of the pastry with a little milk or water. Roll the other half of the pastry into a circle big enough to cover the pie, join the two edges of pastry and trim it. Prick the pastry with a fork, brush it lightly with a little milk to glaze, and bake the pie at Mark 7 (425°) for 20–30 minutes. Serve hot or cold.

JULIA'S FISHCAKES

My sister Julia has looked after many children in her time and these fishcakes are highly thought of by all of them – even the difficult eaters, because it's a good excuse to get out the ketchup bottle and all kids love that!

1 lb. any white fish
½ lb. creamy mashed potatoes
1 chopped onion
Dspn. chopped fresh parsley
1 oz. butter
¼ pt. milk
1 egg beaten
Salt and pepper
A dash of anchovy or Worcester sauce
Crispy breadcrumbs for coating

Simmer the fish gently in the milk, lightly seasoned with salt and pepper, for about 8–10 minutes. At the same time cook the onion in the butter until soft and pale yellow. Drain the liquid from the fish which should be mashed with a fork and then mixed with the potato, onion and parsley. Season it to taste and add the anchovy or Worcester sauce. Allow the mixture to become quite cold, and when it is, shape it into flat fish cakes. Pass them through the beaten egg and then the breadcrumbs and then deep fry them until they are crisp and golden brown.

KEDGEREE

6 oz. rice
8 oz. cooked smoked fish
1 hard-boiled egg, chopped
1 onion, chopped
3 oz. butter
1 dspn. chopped fresh parsley

Cook the rice in boiling salted water until it is cooked through but not mushy, then drain it very well indeed. Chop the onion finely and cook it until golden in 1 ounce of butter. Meanwhile, flake the cooked smoked fish and remove any skin and bones (the best way to cook the fish is to cover it with boiling water and leave it to stand for at least 10 minutes). Mix the egg, fish, onion and parsley into the rice and return it to the pan to reheat. Melt the other 2 ounces of butter, stir it into the Kedgeree, season it to taste and serve it immediately.

MAIN
COURSES

SHOULDER OF LAMB
WITH APRICOT STUFFING

A shoulder of lamb is a delicious cut of meat and if cooked with a stuffing it becomes a very economical family week-end roasting joint. All sorts of stuffings can be used and the one I give here has a real luxury touch to it. Try chopped apple and raisin, sausage meat and onion or whatever takes your fancy. Don't forget to ask the butcher to bone the meat.

1 shoulder of lamb
1 medium onion, finely chopped
1 clove garlic, crushed
¼ lb. dried apricots, chopped
1 eating apple, cored and chopped
1 dspn. soft white breadcrumbs
1 oz. fat for frying
Salt and pepper

To make the stuffing, fry the onion and garlic in the fat until soft then mix them with all the other ingredients. Spread this mixture over the inside of the meat, roll it up and tie it securely with thin string. Roast the joint in the normal way for about 1½ hours, oven temperature Mark 6 (400°), basting the meat regularly and turning it over once or twice.

BEST END OF NECK OF LAMB
WITH ROSEMARY AND GARLIC

2 chops per person
3 cloves garlic, sliced
4 tblspns. oil
2–3 small sprigs fresh rosemary
Or:
2 tspns. dried rosemary
Salt and pepper

Ask the butcher to divide the best end of neck into separate chops. Put the chops and all the other ingredients in a mixing bowl and leave them for at least half an hour. Turn the chops over a couple of times so that each chop is well covered with the oil and the flavour of the garlic and rosemary can impregnate the meat.

Then grill the chops under a hot grill for 8–10 minutes, turning once until the fat is a good crisp deep golden brown. Spoon the juices over the chops a couple of times while they are cooking so they remain really juicy.

A delicious accompaniment to chops cooked this way is a tomato and mint salad. Chump chops are good cooked this way, too, but take a little longer to grill.

MINCED LAMB AND DATE MEATBALLS

$\frac{1}{2}$ pkt. compressed dates, finely chopped
1 clove garlic, crushed
1 small onion, finely chopped
$\frac{1}{2}$ tspn. ground cumin
$\frac{1}{2}$ tspn. powdered cinnamon
Salt and pepper
2 slices white bread
1 tblspn. water
Flour
Oil for frying
1 oz. chopped almonds (optional)
1 lb. minced lamb – either the meat from some
    scrag end or breast of lamb

Soak the bread, without its crusts, in the water. Mix together the minced meat, dates, garlic, onion, spices, salt and pepper and nuts, if they are being used. Then mix in enough of the dampened bread to make the meat mixture pleasantly light. Roll the mixture into small balls, the size of walnuts, roll them in a little flour, then fry them very gently in the oil until golden brown all over. If they are cooked too fast these meatballs will stick to the frying pan.

Serve the meatballs with rice and a crisp green salad – also a small carton of natural yoghurt with some finely chopped onion and cucumber into it.

BREAST OF LAMB WITH SAUSAGEMEAT AND RAISIN STUFFING

1 large breast of lamb
1 medium onion, chopped
½–¾ lb. sausagemeat
2 oz. raisins or sultanas
1 tspn. finely chopped parsley
Salt and pepper
Fat for roasting

Ask the butcher to bone the breast of lamb, then cut away any excess fat and peel off the thick inner skin. Make the stuffing by mixing together all the ingredients, except the roasting fat; spread the stuffing over the inside of the meat, then roll it up and tie it securely with thin string. Roast in the usual way for about 1–1½ hours at Mark 4 (350°), basting regularly.

BREAST OF LAMB WITH YOGHURT AND FRESH GINGER

Fresh ginger is easily obtainable nowadays from any Asian grocery store. As it can be rather fibrous, it is best chopped very finely indeed with a very sharp little knife.

1 breast of lamb
1 eating apple, cored and chopped
1 medium onion, finely chopped
1 clove garlic, crushed
1 tspn. fresh ginger, finely chopped
1 oz. raisins or sultanas
1 small carton natural yoghurt
Salt and pepper
1 tblspn. runny honey (optional)

Ask the butcher to bone the breast of lamb, then cut away any excess fat and peel off the thick inner skin. Make the stuffing by mixing together all the ingredients except the honey, then spread the mixture over the inside of the meat, roll it up and tie it securely with thin string. If possible leave the meat to stand for some time, at least one hour, before cooking it – the flavour will be much nicer. Roast the meat in the usual way for about 1–1½ hours in an oven set at Mark 4 (350°), basting regularly. As an optional extra, add the honey to the juices in the pan about 20 minutes before the meat is ready and keep basting.

LAMB AND TOMATO CASSEROLE

2 lb. scrag end of lamb
2 onions, chopped
1 medium tin tomatoes
4 carrots, cut into rings
1–2 sticks celery, cut into pieces
1 clove garlic, crushed
1 stock cube, dissolved in ½ pt. water
4 oz. seasoned flour
Worcester sauce
2 oz. dripping

Fry the onions and garlic in the fat in a casserole until they are transparent, then remove them from the pan and keep them warm. Roll the meat in the seasoned flour, then fry it in the casserole until each piece is golden brown. Remove the meat from the casserole, and keep it warm. Add the remaining flour to the fat in the pan, fry it gently for 2 minutes then add the tomatoes, and the stock. Bring this to boiling point, then add the onions, meat, the other vegetables and a drop or two of Worcester sauce. Cover the pan and simmer gently on a low heat for 2 hours.

LAMB CASSEROLE WITH HARICOT BEANS

Any of the less expensive cuts of lamb are ideal for this casserole; either scrag end, middle end of neck or chump ends. If he has not already done so, ask the butcher to cut the meat into large chunks ready for cooking.

2 lb. stewing lamb
2 large onions, chopped
2 large carrots, cut into rings
1 clove garlic, crushed
4 oz. dried haricot beans
1 medium tin tomatoes
1 tspn. mixed dried herbs
1 oz. dripping or fat for frying
Salt and pepper

Soak the beans for 12 hours, or overnight, in cold water, then simmer them gently in salted water for 1 hour. Meanwhile, trim the meat, if necessary, and then brown it in the dripping in a casserole pot. Add the onions and garlic and continue the cooking until they are lightly browned as well. Pour on the tomatoes, add the drained beans, the carrots, herbs and seasoning. Cover the pot with foil, then the lid and cook gently on the top of the stove for 1½–2 hours, so that the meat and beans are tender. Like all casseroles this dish can be prepared in advance and gently reheated when necessary.

LAMB AND FRUIT HOT-POT

This is another recipe for using the cheaper cuts of lamb – either scrag end, middle end of neck or chump ends. Personally, I prefer scrag end because it is so meaty.

1½ lb. stewing lamb
2 large onions
1 large apple
1 lb. old potatoes
4 oz. dried prunes
½ pt. water
1 oz. butter
1 oz. dripping
Salt and pepper

If he hasn't already done so, ask the butcher to cut the meat into pieces ready for cooking. Soak the prunes in the water overnight, slice the onions and fry them gently for a few minutes in the fat, remove them from the pan and keep them warm. Season the meat pieces then fry them in the fat until they are well browned on either side. In a fireproof casserole put layers of onions, meat, prunes and sliced, cored apple, then pour over the juice in which the prunes were soaking. Slice the peeled potatoes into ¼-inch rings, and lay them over the contents of the casserole. Sprinkle the potatoes with salt and pepper and dot with little pieces of butter then cover the casserole and bake it for 1½–2 hours in a moderate oven, Mark 4 (350°). Half an hour before serving, remove the lid from the casserole and allow the potatoes to brown.

LAMB STEW WITH DUMPLINGS

1½–2 lb. stewing lamb
2 oz. dripping
2 large onions
3 carrots
2 tomatoes
3 tblspns. flour
1 pt. stock
1 bay leaf
Salt and pepper
Pinch of thyme

For the Dumplings

8 oz. self-raising flour
4 oz. suet, minced
1 teacupful cold water
Pinch salt

For the Stew

Mix the salt, pepper and thyme into the flour, then coat the
pieces of meat with it. Meanwhile, slice the onions, fry them
in the fat in a frying pan until golden brown, then remove
them from the pan. Brown the lamb pieces in the fat and
when they are a good colour, remove them from the pan
and keep them warm. Add to the fat in the pan any remaining flour and fry it a little so that it goes brown but doesn't
burn. Pour on the stock, mixing it carefully with the
browned flour so that lumps do not form and allow it to
boil up. Transfer the onions, meat, gravy from the pan and
all other ingredients for the stew to a casserole pot and cook
in the oven for 1½–2 hours at Mark 3 (325°), or simmer it
on the top of the stove for the same length of time. Twenty

minutes before the stew is ready, correct the seasoning and add the dumplings and continue to cook the stew, making sure that the casserole pot is tightly covered.

To Make the Dumplings

Sift the flour and salt together and mix the minced suet in thoroughly then mix in enough water to make a fairly firm dough. Divide the mixture into walnut-sized pieces, roll them into balls and add to the stew. If the dumplings are bigger, remember that they will take longer to cook.

PORK 'N' BEANS

The combination of pork and beans means a very filling and economical dish. It is also very versatile because so many different things can be cooked with it. This recipe includes black treacle, which gives the traditional sweet flavour, but it is possible to leave that out and use cheap bacon cuts, or pork sausages, tinned tomatoes and extra onions and garlic – the results will be equally tasty.

12 oz. haricot beans
1 lb. belly pork
1 large onion
4 tblspns. black treacle
3 tblspns. tomato purée
2 tspns. mustard powder
1½ pt. hot water
Salt and pepper

Soak the beans for 12 hours, or overnight in cold water. Cut the rind from the pork and cut it into 1-inch pieces. Chop the onion. Mix all the ingredients in a large casserole with the boiling water and cook for 5–6 hours in a low oven or on a low heat on the top of the stove. Keep the pot tightly covered, but give the contents a stir from time to time. This dish is ideal for reheating and can be made in advance and kept in the fridge or a cool place until needed. If reheating it, it may be necessary to add a little more water.

SCRUMPY PORK

$1\frac{1}{2}$–2 lb. cheap cut of pork cut into cubes
1 pt. cider
1 small onion, sliced
2 leeks, cut into rings
4 carrots, cut into rings
1 oz. fat for frying
Seasoned flour
Sprig of rosemary

Fry the onion gently in the fat until it is a pale golden colour. Roll the meat in the seasoned flour and fry it in the pot with the onions. Pour over the cider, add the vegetables and rosemary and cook the casserole in a low oven – Mark 2 (300°) – for about 3 hours. This will taste even better if cooked the day before it is to be eaten and gently reheated.

PORK AND POTATO BAKE

1 lb. belly pork cut into slices
1 very large onion
3 large old potatoes
1 tspn. dried sage or rosemary
1 pt. stock
A little dripping for frying
$\frac{1}{2}$ oz. butter
Salt and pepper

63

Slice the onion and fry it gently in the fat until golden and soft. Remove it from the pan and keep it warm. Fry the pork strips until golden brown on each side. Peel and slice the potatoes, then put half of them in a layer in a greased fireproof dish. Put half the onion on top, then the pork slices, sprinkled with salt and pepper and the dried herb. Cover the pork with the rest of the fried onion and then the rest of the potatoes. Pour over the stock, dot the top with the butter cut into tiny pieces, cover the pot with grease-proof paper or foil, lightly buttered to prevent it sticking, and bake it for 1 hour in a medium oven, Mark 4 (350°). Remove the covering and continue to cook for half an hour so that the potatoes become golden and crispy on top.

PORK SPARERIBS IN TOMATO SAUCE

2 lb. pork ribs
1 large onion
1 tblspn. sultanas
4 tblspns. tomato ketchup
1 tblspn. vinegar
1 tblspn. sugar (preferably demerara)
2 tblspns. water
$\frac{1}{2}$ tspn. mustard powder
Salt and pepper
Little fat for frying

Divide the spareribs into pieces of 2–3 bones each and season them with salt and pepper. Chop the onion and fry it until soft and golden yellow. Combine all the other ingredients and heat them gently in a saucepan until the sugar has melted. Lay the ribs in a shallow fireproof dish with the onions, then pour over the hot sauce. Cover and bake in a moderate oven – Mark 4 (350°) – for about 1 hour, so that the meat is tender and comes away from the bones fairly easily. The spareribs are eaten in the fingers and served with boiled rice and a large box of paper hankies!

FRENCH COLD BEEF SALAD

This is a lovely easy way to make a dish from some cold left-over beef – either roasted or pot roasted. The ingredients are much the same as one would use for a plateful of beef salad – just differently arranged.

Enough cold beef for 4 people – cut into 'soldiers'
4 tomatoes sliced
1 lb. cooked and sliced cold potatoes –
  preferably new ones
Salt and pepper
French dressing

Lay some of the sliced tomatoes in a dish, seasoned with a little salt and pepper, then cover with a layer of beef 'soldiers', then sliced potatoes, and so on until all the ingredients are used up. Then pour on about 2 tablespoonfuls of french dressing – enough to reach each layer but not so much that everything is swimming in oil and vinegar.

BRISKET IN THE POT

There are two ways of cooking this dish – either leaving the piece of rolled brisket whole, or cutting it into chunks as one would normally do for a beef casserole. Using the latter method I have substituted the cheaper cut of flank of beef for the brisket, with excellent results.

1½–2 lb. chosen meat
4 tblspns. oil
4 tblspns. vinegar
2 carrots, sliced
2 onions, chopped
2 bay leaves

8 black peppercorns
6 cloves
½ tspn. dried thyme
1 tspn. brown sugar
1 clove garlic, sliced
4 oz. smoked bacon bits
Salt
1 tblspn. dripping

The meat needs to be 'marinated' overnight – in other words, left in the liquids with the spices so that it soaks up all the flavours. The best way to do that is to put it in a polythene bag with all the ingredients except the bacon, the dripping and one onion. Next day cut the bacon into pieces and fry it gently with the fresh onion. Take the meat from the polythene bag, drain it well, then fry it until browned all over in the dripping. When the meat is ready, add all the other ingredients from the polythene bag, then put everything into a casserole with a tight-fitting lid. Leave the meat to cook in a low oven – Mark 3 (325°) – at the highest, for as long as possible. Long slow cooking is essential if the meat is to be really tender and to taste its best. When the meat is ready, skim the layer of fat off the top of the casserole. If a piece of whole rolled brisket has been used, remove it from the sauce, slice it and serve it with the juice and vegetables poured over. This dish is well worth the time spent cooking it – the aroma when the pot is opened is quite something.

HUNGARIAN GOULASH

1½ lb. stewing beef, cut into cubes
2 large onions, sliced
2 dspns. paprika
1 tspn. caraway seeds
1 tblspn. tomato purée

2 oz. fat for frying
1 beef stock cube dissolved in ¾ pt. water
Salt and pepper

Fry the onions in the fat until they are a pale golden colour then add the tomato purée and the paprika and mix them all together. Then add the meat, cook it a little, then add all the other ingredients. Give everything a good stir, cover the pot and cook the goulash in the oven – Mark 3 (325°) – for 1½–2 hours, or until the meat is tender. Nice and easy! Serve with either boiled rice or pasta – vegetables really aren't necessary.

OXTAIL STEW WITH TOMATO PURÉE

The cooking time for oxtail is rather long, but to taste its best it needs long slow cooking. At its best it is delicious, so it is worth it.

2–3 lb. oxtail pieces
2 large onions, chopped
6 carrots, sliced into rings
2 sticks celery, cut into pieces
1 tspn. mixed herbs
Seasoned flour
2 oz. fat for frying
1 beef stock cube dissolved in ¾ pt. water
2 tblspns. tomato purée
Dash of Worcester sauce

Fry the onions gently in the fat until transparent, remove them from the pan and keep them warm. Cover each piece of oxtail with seasoned flour, fry them briskly until well browned on each side then put them in a casserole pot with all the other ingredients. Give the stew a good stir then cover the pot with foil and then the lid so that the pot is really tightly covered. Cook in the oven for a long time – either overnight at the lowest setting, or for about 4–5 hours at Mark 2 (300°). Serve with creamy mashed potatoes and don't forget the extra plate on the table for the bones!

SAVOURY POT ROAST

2 lb. rolled brisket
1 green pepper, sliced
1 large onion, chopped
1 clove garlic, crushed
1 large tin tomatoes
1 bay leaf
2 oz. dripping
Salt and pepper

Season the meat with some salt and pepper then sear it all over with the dripping in a very hot pan. The meat should be well browned all over if it is to remain nice and juicy. Put it into a casserole with all the other ingredients, cover it and cook it in the oven for at least 3 hours at Mark 3 (325°), or until the meat is tender. Alternatively, cook it over a very low heat on the top of the cooker for the same length of time.

CHICKEN STUFFED WITH OATMEAL

This is a Scottish dish. I was a bit sceptical about it until I'd tried it but now I love it. If the proportions for the stuffing are doubled or trebled, there is enough to stuff a turkey, which is extremely economical for a very large family and makes a nice change at Christmas time.

8 oz. medium oatmeal
4 oz. suet, finely minced
2 medium onions, finely chopped
Salt and plenty of black pepper
1 chicken for 4 people
Fat for roasting

Mix the oatmeal, suet, onions and seasoning and pack it into the chicken. Roast the chicken in the normal way – the time depends on its size. Serve with the usual vegetables and gravy, though potatoes aren't really necessary.

CRISPY FRIED CHICKEN WITH SPICED APPLE RINGS

For 4 people either buy a 2½-pound roasting chicken, or 4 chicken pieces, or 8 drumsticks – it all depends on which is the best buy. If frying the chicken for a party or a picnic, drumsticks are probably the best because they are the easiest to eat in the fingers.

Chosen chicken for 4 people
2 beaten eggs
3 oz. flour seasoned with salt, pepper, onion or
**   garlic**
Salt
¼ tspn. ground ginger
Breadcrumbs for coating

For the Apple Rings

1 large or 2 small firm eating apples, cored and
**   cut into rings**

**1 oz. demerara sugar mixed with $\frac{1}{4}$ tspn. dry
mustard**
$\frac{1}{4}$ tspn. ground cloves and a pinch of nutmeg
2 oz. butter for frying

To Cook the Chicken

The chicken is to be fried in deep fat, so while that is heating
up, pass each piece through the seasoned flour, then the
beaten egg and finally coat them with breadcrumbs. When
the hot fat has a fine haze rising from it – not smoke! – put
in the chicken pieces and cook them for a good minute.
Then turn off the heat under the pan and let them continue
to cook for a further 8–10 minutes so that they are golden
brown and cooked right through.

Remove the pieces from the fat and drain them on some
kitchen paper before serving them with the apple rings,
which are cooked while the chicken is frying.

To Cook the Apple Rings

Cover the apple rings, which must have their peel left on,
with the spicy sugar. Fry them for a couple of minutes each
side in the butter. They will be golden brown and sticky and
the juice in the pan should be poured over them.

CHICKEN ROASTED WITH TARRAGON

Cold chicken is a great summer stand-by – easy to cook and
not too expensive. One of the loveliest flavours of summer is
a chicken cooked with fresh tarragon inside – the result is
chicken with a gentle herby flavour and it's a great improve-
ment for deep-frozen chickens. Most greengrocers will sell
fresh tarragon and it is always possible to buy it in London
markets.

$2\frac{1}{2}$–3 lb. roasting chicken
1 bunch fresh tarragon

1 oz. butter
Salt and pepper
Extra ounce of butter for roasting

Sprinkle the salt and pepper inside the cavity of the chicken. Chop the tarragon very finely and mash it into the 2 ounces of butter. Put that inside the chicken too. Then roast the chicken in the usual way with the 1 ounce of butter, spooning the juices over it regularly so that it stays moist and juicy. Serve the chicken hot with the herby juices poured over, or cold, very thinly sliced.

CHICKEN RISOTTO

I think I've said quite enough in the introduction about what can go into a risotto. The method of cooking I give here is not the classic one, but it will give a tasty dish anyway.

2 oz. uncooked rice per person
1 large onion, chopped
1 clove garlic, crushed
1 tblspn. cooked peas
2 oz. sliced mushrooms or mushroom stalks
Chicken left-overs, chopped
2 tomatoes, chopped
$\frac{1}{2}$ chicken stock cube in $\frac{3}{4}$ pt. hot water
1 oz. fat for frying

Cook the rice according to the directions on the packet – do not overcook it or the risotto will be a savoury but gluey mess. Fry the onion and garlic in the fat until golden brown then add all the other ingredients to the pan. Cook gently until practically all the liquid has evaporated, add the cooked rice, allow it to become really hot and serve it immediately.

One of the nicest accompaniments to chicken risotto is a crisp green salad with french dressing.

CHICKEN CASSEROLE WITH CIDER

1 chicken or chicken pieces
1 small bottle cider
2 onions, chopped
3–4 carrots, cut into rings
2 sticks celery, cut into pieces
2 tomatoes
1 clove garlic, crushed
½ tspn. dried mixed herbs
Flour for coating
Salt and pepper
2 oz. fat for frying

Cut the chicken into pieces, season the flour with the salt and pepper and herbs and coat the chicken pieces with it. Fry the onion and garlic until soft, remove them from the pan and keep them warm. Fry the floured chicken pieces until they are deep golden brown all over, remove them from the pan and put them in a casserole with the onions to keep warm. Pour the cider into the hot pan, stirring in all the bits left from the frying, let it boil up then add it to the chicken. Peel and chop the other vegetables, add them to the casserole and cook it in a moderate oven – Mark 4 (350°) – for 1–1¼ hours, until the chicken is tender. Before serving, check the seasoning and serve with boiled rice or noodles.

CHICKEN WITH HONEY AND THYME

This dish can be made with chicken quarters, wings or drumsticks, or turkey drumsticks or wings. The cooking time given here is for chicken quarters, but, obviously, will be more or less if drumsticks or wings are used.

4 chicken quarters
2–3 tblspns. runny honey
Juice 1 large lemon
1 tspn. dried thyme or 2–3 sprigs fresh thyme
Salt and pepper
2 oz. butter

Melt the butter in a pan and fry the chicken in it until it is well browned all over, remove it from the pan and put it into a casserole to keep warm. Mix the honey, lemon and thyme in a saucepan, and over a low heat, bring it to the boil. Pour the honey sauce over the chicken, cover the casserole and bake it in a moderate oven – Mark 5 (375°) – for 20–30 minutes.

KOORMA CURRY

Most people like curries and they really are very simple to make. They can also be very inexpensive because the cheaper cuts of meat are ideal for currying. I usually use breast of lamb for this Koorma, but I have also used belly of pork and chicken. All of the spices, etc., can be bought very easily in Asian grocers' shops and once someone has cooked their own curry, I guarantee they will do so again and again. Incidentally, the flavour of this particular dish is even better if it is cooked the day before it is to be eaten and then reheated.

2 cartons unsweetened natural yoghurt
½ pkt. creamed coconut
4 cloves

3 cardomoms
1–2 big black cardomoms
½ tspn. turmeric
½ tspn. chilli powder
Or:
¼ tspn. finely chopped fresh chilli
¼ tspn. chopped fresh ginger
1 clove garlic, crushed
1 dspn. vindaloo paste
2 onions, chopped
2–3 pieces cinnamon bark
Or:
½ tspn. powdered cinnamon
3 lb. chosen meat
Salt
Squeeze of lemon juice
2 oz. fat for frying

Cook the onion and garlic in a casserole pot in the fat until golden brown, then add the meat and spices, mix well and continue to cook for 4–5 minutes. Add all the other ingredients, mix thoroughly, then cook the curry in a low oven, or on a low heat for as long as possible – until the meat is tender.

COCONUT EGG CURRY

1 lb. tomatoes *or* 1 tin tomatoes
1 tbspn. ground almonds
1 tspn. chilli powder
Or:
¼ tspn. chopped fresh chilli
1 tspn. turmeric
1 tspn. ground coriander

¼ tspn. ground ginger
2 oz. creamed coconut
½ pt. water
1 large onion, chopped
1 clove garlic, crushed
1 dspn. cornflour
8 hard-boiled eggs
Salt
Fat for frying

Cook the tomatoes in the water until they are very soft, then mix them to purée with a wooden spoon. Fry the onion and garlic until pale golden brown, add the nuts and spices and fry them until well browned. Add the tomato purée and the coconut and bring to the boil. Mix the cornflour with a spoonful of cold water, remove the pan from the heat and gradually add the cornflour. Return the pan to a low heat and simmer the sauce for 30 minutes. Halve the eggs, add them to the sauce and continue cooking for 5 minutes, very gently, so that the eggs are heated through but not broken.

If using tinned tomatoes, cook them in their own juice and omit the water.

LAMBS' TONGUES WITH ONION SAUCE

4 lamb's tongues
1 carrot
1 piece parsley
2 large onions
1 oz. flour
2 oz. butter
¼ pt. milk
Salt and pepper
1 bay leaf
1 small onion

Put the lamb's tongues in a pot with the carrot, parsley, bay leaf and small onion and cover them with water. Slowly bring the water to the boil, skim off any froth which may form on top, add a cupful of cold water, then simmer the tongues for 1½ hours. To make the sauce, chop the onions finely and cook them in a covered pan with 1 ounce of the butter, melted, until they are very soft. In a separate pan, melt the other 1 ounce of butter, add the flour and cook it for 2–3 minutes, stirring constantly. Remove the pan from the heat, and gradually mix in the milk, stirring to prevent lumps forming. Return the pan to the heat, add the cooked onions and gently bring the sauce to boiling point. Cook it for 3–4 minutes, still stirring, then season it to taste. When the tongues are cooked, remove them from the liquid and skin them. Cut them into slices longways and serve them with the sauce poured over.

LAMBS' TONGUES WITH ONIONS AND TOMATOES

4 lamb's tongues
1 carrot
1 piece parsley
1 large onion
4 large tomatoes *or* 1 small tin tomatoes
Salt and pepper
2 oz. grated cheese
1 oz. fat for frying
1 bay leaf
1 small onion

Cook the tongues as described in the previous recipe.

To Make the Sauce

Chop the onions, and fry them gently in the chosen fat until transparent. Skin the tomatoes, chop them and add them to the onions, then cook both until the tomatoes are soft, seasoning to taste. When the tongues are cooked, skin and slice them and lay them in a greased fireproof dish. Pour the sauce over them, sprinkle the cheese on top and grill until the cheese is bubbly and golden brown.

LIVER WITH ORANGE SAUCE

All too often liver is cooked so long that it resembles old boot leather, which is a great pity. To prevent the necessity of cooking it for a long time, it is worth buying liver in the piece from the butcher and slicing it really thinly at home with a very sharp knife. The slices will probably turn out to be very small indeed, but the liver will be much nicer when cooked.

1 lb. liver
¼ lb. streaky bacon or bacon bits
1 medium onion, chopped
Juice of 2 large oranges
Seasoned flour
A little extra fat for frying
Salt and pepper

Chop the bacon and put it in a frying pan over a low heat until the fat begins to run, then add the chopped onion and fry it until it is golden yellow. Remove the onion and bacon from the pan and keep them warm. Roll the liver slices in seasoned flour and fry them gently for about 1–2 minutes, using a little extra fat if necessary. If the liver is really thinly sliced, it won't take longer to cook and will remain lovely and juicy. Remove the liver from the pan and keep it warm. Add the orange juice to the pan, scraping in all the bits left from the frying, bring it to boiling point and allow the sauce to bubble for 2–3 minutes. Season it to taste. Lay the onion and bacon in a serving dish, lay the liver on top and pour over it the strained sauce. Serve with creamed potatoes.

LIVER WITH LEMON AND SAGE

1 lb. liver
Seasoned flour
2 oz. butter
1 tspn. finely chopped sage
1 clove garlic
Juice of 1 large lemon

Buy the liver in a piece and slice it as described in the previous recipe, then roll the slices in the seasoned flour. Crush the garlic clove and put it into a frying pan with the butter and sage. When the butter is beginning to bubble, fry the liver on each side for 1–2 minutes, then remove it and lay it in a serving dish. Pour the lemon juice into the pan, allow it to boil up and pour it immediately over the liver. This is also a delicious way to cook kidneys – slice them and coat them with flour exactly as for the liver, but cook them for a little longer – making sure they don't go hard and rubbery either.

TRIPE IN TOMATO SAUCE

The best tripe looks like honeycomb and should be a pale creamy colour.

1 lb. honeycomb tripe
1 onion, finely chopped
1 oz. butter or margarine
2 oz. bacon pieces

1 carrot, finely diced
2 level tblspns. flour
1 tblspn. tomato purée
1 chicken stock cube, dissolved in ¾ pt. water
1 tspn. lemon juice
2 oz. mushrooms, sliced or mushroom stalks
Salt and pepper

Put the tripe in a pot, cover it with cold water and slowly bring it to the boil. Strain away the water and cut the tripe into 2–3-inch pieces. Gently fry the bacon, onion and carrot in the butter until the onion is soft. Then add the flour and continue to cook the mixture until the flour is a good brown nutty colour but not burnt at all. Then add all the other ingredients, except the tripe, and bring the sauce to the boil. Add the tripe and simmer everything for about 1½ hours. Serve with creamed potatoes or buttered shell noodles.

ROAST HEARTS

This is a recipe given to me by my Scottish friend Mary Ransome, exactly as she wrote it down for me.

Sheep's hearts are quite inexpensive and very succulent. They make a nice change to the usual, more expensive meat dishes. One or two hearts per person, depending on appetite.

4 sheep's hearts
2 tblspns. breadcrumbs
1 tspn. chopped parsley
1 tspn. shredded suet
Salt and pepper
A little milk
Dripping

Mix the breadcrumbs, seasoning, suet and parsley. Bind with a little milk. Wash the hearts, cut away the pipes and

79

dividing walls. Stuff the hearts, fold the flaps over and skewer. Heat dripping in a strong pan. Put the hearts in and brown. Reduce heat and cook gently for about 1 hour or a little more. Turn the hearts occasionally. Lift the hearts out when done, strain most of the fat out of the pan, leaving some residue. Make the gravy in this with vegetable water, a little browning and a little thickening.

Just let me add that Mary's stuffed roast hearts are marvellous!

TOAD-IN-THE-HOLE

Instead of always using sausages for Toad-in-the-Hole, try using up slices of cold cooked meat, thick fingers of tinned luncheon meat, or halved kidneys, which have been slightly pre-cooked. All sorts of things make good 'toads'.

1 lb. sausages
6 oz. flour
1 pt. milk
2 eggs
Salt and pepper

Skin the sausages and lay them in a greased fireproof dish. Make a batter from the other ingredients by sifting the flour, salt and pepper into a mixing bowl. Make a well in the middle and break the egg into the well, add 2 tablespoonfuls of milk and gradually, mixing from the middle, draw in the flour. Add more milk from time to time until all the flour is mixed in, then all the milk. The batter should be free from lumps and well beaten so that it will be nice and light when cooked. Pour the batter over the sausages and bake it in a moderate oven – Mark 4 (350°) – for 1–1½ hours, or until the batter is well risen and golden brown.

SAUSAGEMEAT AND CABBAGE BAKE

1 medium-sized white cabbage
1 lb. sausagemeat
2 large onions
4 tblspns. tomato ketchup
1 tblspn. vinegar
1 dspn. brown sugar
4 tblspns. water
Salt and pepper
1 oz. fat for frying

Chop the onions and fry them gently in the fat until soft and
golden yellow. Cut the cabbage into thin strips, discarding
the stalks and cook it in boiling salted water for 3–4 minutes.
Then drain the cabbage thoroughly. Into a greased fireproof
dish, put layers of cabbage, cooked onion and sausagemeat,
seasoning each layer lightly with salt and pepper, and
finishing with a layer of cabbage. In a saucepan mix together
the ketchup, water, vinegar and sugar and bring them to the
boil. Stir the sauce until the sugar has dissolved then pour
it over the sausagemeat and cabbage. Cover the dish and
bake in a moderate oven – Mark 4 (350°) – so that the
cabbage is cooked through.

SALLY'S SAUSAGE ROLL

1 small pkt. puff pastry
1 lb. sausagemeat
1 hard-boiled egg, chopped
1 medium onion, chopped
1 tspn. mixed herbs
Salt and pepper
Milk to glaze

Roll the pastry out to an oblong. Mix together all the other ingredients, except the milk, roll them into a sausage shape and lay it on the pastry. Roll up the pastry, moistening the edges so that they stick firmly, and lay the sausage-roll on a baking sheet, join side underneath. Brush over with a little milk to glaze and bake it in a hot oven – Mark 7 (450°) – for 25–30 minutes, so that the pastry is a good golden colour.

SAUSAGE AND MARROW FRITTERS

6 large pork sausages
8 slices marrow

Fritter Batter

4 oz. plain flour
2 egg yolks
1 tblspn. oil
$\frac{1}{4}$ pt. milk
Pinch of salt
1 egg white

To Make the Batter

Sift the flour with the salt into a bowl, make a well in the centre and put the egg yolks and oil into it. Gradually incorporating the flour into the egg yolks, mix to a batter, adding the milk bit by bit. Leave the batter in a cool place for at least half an hour and just before using whip the egg white until stiff and fold it into the batter. Cook the sausages, cut them in half and skin them. Remove the pips and fibres from the middle of the marrow rings and put them into boiling salted water for 1 minute, then drain them thoroughly. Dip the sausage and marrow pieces into the batter and deep fry them in hot oil until crisp and golden brown.

MEATBALLS IN SPICY SAUCE

For the Meatballs
1 lb. minced beef or lamb
4–6 oz. soft white breadcrumbs
1 medium onion
1 egg
Salt and pepper
Dash of Worcester sauce
A little fat for frying
Flour

For the Sauce
3 tblspns. tomato purée
1 tblspn. brown sugar
1 tblspn. vinegar
$\frac{1}{4}$ pt. hot water
$\frac{1}{4}$ tspn. ginger powder

To Make the Meatballs
Beat the egg and chop the onion very finely. Mix together the meat and breadcrumbs, then the onion and finally the beaten egg. Season and add a little Worcester sauce. Roll spoonfuls of the mixture into balls, coat them lightly in flour, then fry them gently until golden brown. Cook them in the sauce, simmering them in a covered pan, for about half an hour.

To Make the Sauce
Mix all the ingredients together in a saucepan, bring the sauce to the boil and stir until the sugar has dissolved.

LEFT-OVER MEAT ROLL

$\frac{1}{2}$–$\frac{3}{4}$ lb. cooked meat, minced
1 medium onion, chopped
1 tspn. chopped parsley
2 tblspns. tomato ketchup or brown sauce or gravy
Salt and pepper
1 small pkt. frozen pastry

Roll the pastry out to an oblong. Mix all the other ingredients together and place the mixture in an oblong on the centre of the pastry. Fold the pastry over, moistening the edges so that they stick together firmly, and seal the ends as well. Place the roll on a baking sheet, join side underneath, brush it over with a little milk to glaze and bake it in a hot oven – Mark 7 (425°) – for about 25 minutes, or until the pastry is a good golden brown.

SKIRLEY

Another of Mary Ransome's Scottish recipes, as she wrote it down. The given quantities should serve four people.

4 oz. medium oatmeal
1 medium-size onion
2 oz. good beef dripping
Salt and pepper to taste

Cook the sliced onion in hot dripping until golden. Add the oatmeal and condiments. Mix well together then continue cooking slowly with the lid on for about 15 minutes. Serve hot with mashed potato. Stir occasionally.

This is a nourishing and filling dish, yet tasty. It is most economical. When butcher meat is scarce or expensive even the menfolk will be quite satisfied with a good meal of

Skirley. It is particularly acceptable in cold weather. One can just imagine this dish being invented by some poor but thrifty Scottish crofter, in the days of yesteryear, on some rugged Scottish island in the depths of a bitter winter with mountainous waves lashing the shores, deep snowdrifts on the ground and all contact with the mainland cut off. Skirley is as good today as it was then. What more can one say?

RABBIT CASSEROLE WITH BACON AND CIDER

Rabbit is a delicious meat, and there are many lovely country-style recipes for using it which are not very expensive. I prefer to buy a whole rabbit fresh from the butcher, rather than frozen pieces – after all, the butcher will skin and prepare it for you and some butchers do sell rabbits cheaply – but for this casserole the pieces are very good.

Rabbit sufficient for 4 people
$\frac{1}{2}$ pt. cider
$\frac{1}{4}$ lb. bacon pieces or streaky bacon
2 onions chopped
4 carrots, cut into rings
1 clove garlic, crushed
Seasoned flour
Little extra fat for frying
1 oz. raisins or sultanas (optional)
1 tspn. chopped parsley

Fry the chopped bacon gently, then when the fat runs, add the onion and garlic and fry them until they are golden yellow. Remove the bacon and onion from the pan and keep them warm. Roll the rabbit pieces in the seasoned flour and fry them until they are golden brown all over. Take them from the pan, keep them warm and add 1 tablespoonful of seasoned flour to the pan and let it frizzle for a minute or so. Pour in the cider and let it come to the boil. Put all the ingredients into a casserole, pour over the cider sauce and cover the pan tightly. Simmer the casserole on the top of the stove for at least 1½ hours or cook it in the oven at Mark 3 (325°) for 1½–2 hours, until the rabbit is tender. As with most casseroles, this dish will taste even better reheated the next day so it is ideal for making in advance. Serve with creamy mashed potatoes to soak up the delicious juice.

SAUSAGES AND KIDNEYS IN CIDER, WITH RICE

4 pork sausages, cut into pieces
½ lb. kidney, cut into pieces
4 rashers bacon or ¼ lb. bacon bits
1 large onion, chopped
1 wineglass cider
1 tspn. chopped parsley
Salt and pepper
1 or 2 tomatoes, chopped (optional)
6 oz. rice, cooked according to the instructions on the packet

While the rice is cooking, fry the bacon on a low heat, and add the onion when the fat begins to run. Fry until golden, then add the sausage and kidney pieces. When they have cooked for 3–4 minutes, add the cider, tomatoes and parsley and continue to cook until the kidneys are cooked through. Serve with the boiled rice.

SAVOURY BACON PUDDING

The full instructions for making steamed puddings are in the pudding section. Savoury puddings such as this one are made in exactly the same way.

8 oz. flour
4 oz. suet, minced
$\frac{1}{2}$ tspn. baking powder
Pinch of salt
$\frac{1}{4}$ pt. cold water
$\frac{1}{2}$ lb. chopped bacon bits
1 large onion, chopped
2 oz. grated cheese

Make a suet crust with the flour, suet, baking powder, salt and water. Chop the bacon and cook it in a pan over a low heat until the fat begins to run. Add the onion and fry it until golden. Mix the bacon, onions and grated cheese into the suet crust, put it in a bowl and steam it for $1\frac{1}{2}$ hours.

SPAGHETTI BOLOGNESE

$\frac{3}{4}$ lb. minced beef
2 tblspns. tomato purée
1 large onion, chopped
1 clove garlic, crushed
1 carrot, finely diced
1 wineglass red wine
1 bay leaf
Salt and pepper
1 oz. fat or oil
Little extra water

Fry the onion and garlic gently in the fat or oil. When they are transparent, add the meat and fry it until it is brown all over and looks crumbly.

Add all the other ingredients, give them a good stir, cover the pan and simmer the sauce slowly for about half an hour, until the carrot is cooked. If the liquid evaporates too much, add a little extra water, enough to give a good juicy gravy. Cook the spaghetti according to the instructions on the packet and serve it in separate dishes with the sauce poured over and a sprinkling of Parmesan cheese.

SPAGHETTI WITH BACON AND PEAS

I once had an Italian friend who made a dinner for me and my friends which I shall never forget. He made fresh pasta in my kitchen which he hung in great strings over a broom-handle balanced between two chairs. I'd never seen fresh pasta being made before and the whole process was happy, domestic and exceedingly appetizing. However, packet pasta will be just as good for this dish – ribbon noodles if you can get them, or spaghetti. In Soho it is possible to buy freshly made pasta – if you do so, take the opportunity to buy fresh Parmesan cheese at the same time.

1 lb. ribbon noodles or spaghetti
½ lb. bacon, cut into thin strips
½ lb. cooked peas
1 clove garlic, crushed
3 oz. butter
1 oz. Parmesan cheese *or* finely grated Cheddar

Cook the noodles in boiling salted water until cooked through but not too soft. Meanwhile, melt 1 ounce of the butter in a frying pan and gently fry the bacon with the garlic. The butter must not become at all browned. Then add the peas and heat them through. When the pasta is ready, drain it thoroughly, return it to the saucepan in which it was cooked and over a very low flame, mix in the bacon and peas, then the 2 ounces of butter cut into tiny pieces and finally the cheese. Stir the pasta until it is thoroughly coated with the butter and cheese. Serve immediately.

NOODLES WITH SURPRISES

Noodles come in many different shapes and sizes, but however they come they are delicious and filling and make excellent cheap meals. The 'surprises' in this recipe are the different things which can be added to a dish of boiled, buttered noodles.

The basics are the pasta, the butter and the cheese, after that it's up to you. Cook about 1 pound of noodles in boiling salted water until they are cooked through but not soggy. The time necessary depends on what type is being used. When the noodles are ready, drain them thoroughly, then return them to the pan with 1 ounce of butter cut into tiny pieces and 4 ounces of grated cheese, and salt and pepper to taste. Stir the noodles gently until the butter and cheese coats each piece thoroughly. If some chopped fresh parsley is added there is already a marvellous supper dish, which is delicious served by itself or with some tomato sauce. However, the addition of some fried onion, or bacon or mushrooms, chopped frankfurter sausages, etc., creates a dish to please practically everyone.

LASAGNE

Another very filling and popular dish, ideal for hungry families or guests.

Meat sauce, cooked as for spaghetti bolognese
1 pt. milk
2 oz. butter or margarine
2 oz. flour
Salt and pepper
Nutmeg
Lasagne leaves
1 oz. grated Cheddar or Parmesan

For the White Sauce

Melt the butter in a saucepan, and add the flour – then cook the flour gently for 2–3 minutes, stirring so that it doesn't burn. Remove the pan from the heat and gradually mix in the milk, stirring to prevent lumps forming. Return the pan to the heat once more and gently bring the sauce to the boil, stirring all the time and let it cook for 2–3 minutes. Season to taste and add quite a lot of grated nutmeg, until you like the flavour, and continue to cook the sauce for another 2–3 minutes. When the sauce is ready fill a greased fireproof dish with layers of meat sauce, lasagne leaves and white sauce, finishing with a layer of white sauce. Sprinkle the cheese over the top and bake in the oven for 20–30 minutes at Mark 5 (375°). Serve immediately. The best accompaniment, if one is wanted that is, is a plain green salad with french dressing.

SPAGHETTI NAPOLITANA

1 lb. spaghetti
½ lb. tomatoes, chopped or 1 small tin tomatoes
1 large onion, chopped
¼ tspn. dried basil or 1 tspn. fresh basil, chopped
1 clove garlic, crushed
½ tspn. sugar (optional)
¼ pt. cider

1 tblspn. oil
Salt and black pepper
2 oz. grated Cheddar cheese or 1 oz. Parmesan

Make the tomato sauce by gently frying the onion and garlic in the oil until transparent. Add all the other ingredients (except the cheese and spaghetti) and cook until the onions and tomatoes are soft and pulpy. Either serve the sauce as it is, poured over the spaghetti, with the cheese sprinkled on top, or put it through a sieve or liquidizer and then pour it over the spaghetti.

MACARONI CHEESE

$\frac{1}{2}$ lb. macaroni
1 pt. cheese sauce made from 2 oz. butter,
** 2 oz. flour, 1 pt. milk and 3 oz. cheese**
1 medium-sized onion, chopped
1–2 tomatoes, chopped
2–3 rashers streaky bacon, chopped or bacon bits
1 oz. grated cheese
1 tbspn. soft white breadcrumbs
Salt and pepper

Cook the macaroni in boiling salted water until just cooked through and then drain it thoroughly. Meanwhile, make the sauce according to the method described in the recipe for lasagne, omitting the nutmeg, and putting in 3 ounces of cheese instead. Fry the bacon until the fat begins to run, add the onion and fry until golden brown. Chop the tomatoes and add all three to the cheese sauce. Mix the macaroni into the sauce and put the lot into a greased fireproof dish. Mix the 1 ounce of cheese and the breadcrumbs together and sprinkle them over the macaroni. Grill under a hot grill until the topping is golden brown and crisp. Serve immediately.

POTATO GNOCCHI (pronounced nocky!)

These are delightfully easy to make and may be served with butter and cheese, tomato or meat sauce as you wish.

1 lb. old potatoes
7 oz. flour
Salt

Boil the potatoes, drain them and mash them thoroughly. Mix into the potatoes the sieved flour and salt to taste, and make a light dough which should not be sticky. When the dough is cool shape it into a long sausage on a floured board and cut it into pieces the size of walnuts. Drop the gnocchi, a few at a time, into a pan of boiling salted water and simmer them for 5–10 minutes. They are cooked when they rise to the surface of the water and should then be lifted out with a spoon and drained.

CANNELLONI

½ lb. cannelloni
Tomato sauce as for spaghetti napolitana
1 lb. spinach
4 oz. cream cheese
1 egg
Salt and pepper
2 oz. grated cheese

Cook the cannelloni in boiling salted water for about 5 minutes, then drain it well. Make the filling by cooking the spinach, draining it and chopping it finely. Mix it with the cream cheese and the egg, well beaten, and season the mixture with salt and pepper. Spoon the filling into the cannelloni and put them into a greased fireproof dish. Pour over the sieved or liquidized tomato sauce, sprinkle the grated cheese on top and bake in a moderate oven – Mark 4 (350°) – for about 30 minutes.

CHEESE AND BACON FLAN

This is an excellent family dish because it is equally good served hot or cold. It is ideal for lunch, supper, picnics or lunch-boxes. Funnily enough it's a dish that people frequently think is difficult to make, until they have made it and then it becomes a stand-by.

8 oz. shortcrust pastry, made from
    8 oz. flour, 4 oz. butter or margarine, pinch of
    salt, water to mix or 1 pkt. frozen pastry
1 onion, chopped
2–3 rashers bacon, chopped
3 eggs
¾ pt. milk
2 oz. grated cheese
Salt and pepper

Roll out the pastry and line a 7- or 8-inch flan tin with it. Fry the onion and bacon together, sprinkle it over the bottom of the flan case, then sprinkle over the grated cheese. Mix the eggs into the milk very thoroughly, and season with salt and pepper. Pour this into the flan case, allowing half an inch clear at the top to allow room for the custard to rise. Bake in a good oven – Mark 6 (400°) – until the custard is firm to the touch in the middle and golden brown all over.

BAKED STUFFED POTATOES WITH CHEESE

Everybody seems to like baked potatoes. Cooked like this they are marvellous to serve with a big bowl of almost any soup and will make a very filling meal. Men can usually eat two potatoes! They can be baked at the very top of the oven while a casserole for the next day is cooking away at the bottom. If being cooked this way, they will take longer to cook because the oven should not be too hot to spoil the casserole.

1 or 2 large old potatoes per person
1 lb. chopped onions
1 oz. grated cheese per potato
1 oz. fat for frying
Salt and pepper
½ oz. butter per potato

Wash, dry and prick the potatoes with a fork and bake them in a hot oven for 1–1½ hours, depending on the size. Fry the onions until golden brown and slightly crisp. When the potatoes are ready, cut them in half longways and scoop out the flesh. Mix the onions and butter into the potato and season it with salt and pepper. Pile the potato back into the skins, sprinkle the cheese on top and grill the potatoes until the cheese is bubbly and golden brown.

BAKED STUFFED ONIONS

Spanish onions are ideal for cooking this way and although I suggest sausagemeat for the stuffing almost any savoury mixture will do. One onion is sufficient for one person, so multiply all the ingredients by the number of people you are cooking for.

1 large Spanish onion
2 oz. sausagemeat
¼ pt. cheese sauce, as per the recipe for
   macaroni cheese

Peel the onions and trim the root end but do not cut it away altogether. Boil the onions in salted water for 10–15 minutes. Remove them from the water and allow them to cool until they are comfortable to handle. When they are, take out the centre with a spoon, chop it, and mix it with the sausagemeat. Pack the stuffing back into the onions, place them in a greased fireproof dish, pour over the cheese sauce and bake for about 30 minutes at an oven temperature of Mark 4 (350°), until the cheese sauce is golden brown and bubbly.

ONION JOHNNIES

Another of Scottish Mary's recipes – again, written as she wrote it for me. This is a 'must' for onion lovers! This is for 6 people.

¾ lb. shortcrust pastry
6 medium-sized onions
12 cloves
Salt and pepper
6 small pieces butter
White sauce
Chopped parsley

Do not use rich shortcrust pastry. A very plain shortcrust pastry is wanted. Roll out the pastry, cut it into 6 pieces and roll each piece into a circle. Place a peeled onion in each circle. Add salt, pepper, a small piece of butter and stick 2 cloves in each onion. Moisten edges of pastry and seal around onions. Put each into a small scalded and floured cloth. Tie securely. Put into a pan of boiling water, boil for about 2 hours, and serve with parsley sauce.

The above is a tasty and filling supper dish and one which can generally be made without rushing out to the shops. It can be a great stand-by if hungry and unexpected guests call on early closing day, and they won't be eating you out of house and home!

SPANISH OMELETTE

The ingredients (apart from the eggs of course!) can be varied – the suggestions given here are fairly basic.

**3 eggs
1 chopped fried onion
1 tblspn. cooked peas
1 slice cooked chopped bacon
Salt and pepper
1 tspn. butter**

Beat the eggs very thoroughly in a bowl and season them with salt and pepper. Melt the butter in a frying pan and swirl it around so that the surface of the pan is well greased. When the butter starts to sizzle pour in the eggs and cook them over a medium heat. As the eggs start to cook, sprinkle in the other ingredients and continue to cook until the eggs are firm but not hard.

ONION SOUFFLÉ

**½ lb. onions, chopped
3 oz. grated cheese
1 oz. butter
1 oz. flour**

$\frac{1}{4}$ pt. milk
4 eggs
Salt and pepper

Cook the onions in the milk until they are very soft. Strain the onions from the liquid, set it aside and put the onions through a sieve or liquidize them. Melt the butter in a saucepan, mix in the flour and cook it for 2–3 minutes, stirring to prevent it burning. Remove the pan from the heat and gradually mix in the onion liquid, stirring constantly so that lumps do not form. Add the cheese, return the pan to the heat, bring the sauce to boiling point, and allow it to bubble gently for 2–3 minutes, stirring all the time. Remove the pan from the heat and mix in the onion purée. Add the egg yolks and season to taste. Whip the egg whites until stiff then fold them into the cheese and onion mixture. Pour the mixture into a greased 8-inch soufflé dish, or other high-sided dish, and bake the soufflé in a moderate oven – Mark 4 (350°) – for about 30 minutes. The soufflé should be well risen, and golden brown on the top.

SPINACH QUICHE

8 oz. shortcrust pastry or 1 pkt. frozen pastry
1 lb. spinach, cooked and drained
1 onion, chopped
2 oz. grated cheese
$\frac{1}{2}$ pt. milk
2 eggs
Salt and pepper

Roll out the pastry and line a 6- or 7-inch flan tin. Fry the onion lightly then sprinkle it over the bottom of the flan. Sprinkle over the cheese and then the spinach. Mix the eggs into the milk well, season with salt and pepper and pour it into the flan. Allow half an inch clear at the top of the flan case to allow the custard to rise. Bake in a good oven – Mark 6 (400°) – until the custard is firm to the touch in the middle and golden brown all over.

SAVOURY BAKED RICE AND CHEESE

6 oz. uncooked rice
1 pt. milk
1 tblspn. butter
1 egg
¼ lb. grated cheese
¼ lb. bacon bits, chopped
1 large onion, chopped

Cook the rice in boiling salted water for about 10 minutes, then drain it thoroughly. Fry the onion until golden brown and the bacon until slightly crisp. Beat the egg then mix together all the ingredients reserving some of the cheese. Put the mixture into a greased fireproof dish, spread the rest of the cheese over the top and bake for about 1 hour in the oven – Mark 4 (350°).

STUFFED PANCAKES IN CHEESE SAUCE

This is one of the ways to use the pancakes, the recipe for which is in the 'Store Cupboard' section. The filling can be anything savoury, such as minced cold meat and onions, or onions, bacon and a few mushrooms, or even left-over risotto – in other words, whatever is available. Allowing 2 pancakes per person, lay the choice of stuffing along the pancake and roll it up. Put the stuffed pancakes in a greased fireproof dish and pour over 1 pint of cheese sauce for 8 pancakes and bake in a moderate oven – Mark 4 (350°) – until the sauce is bubbly and golden on top.

PUDDINGS

CARAMEL ORANGES

1 orange per person
½ pt. water
4 oz. sugar

Peel the oranges round and round with a very sharp little knife, like one does with an apple to see if one can get the peel off in one long spiral. Make sure all the pith is cut off as well. Slice the oranges into thin rings and put them into a serving bowl. Put the sugar into a small saucepan with ¼ pint of the water. Bring it to the boil and let it boil slowly, without stirring, until it turns a rich golden brown colour. Wearing oven-gloves, or with a cloth over each hand, remove the pan from the heat and immediately pour in the other ¼ pint of water. (The cloths are to prevent any little burns from the hot sugar, which will spit when the cold water is poured in.) Return the pan to a low heat and stir until the thick caramel has completely dissolved. Pour the sugar mixture over the oranges and chill in the fridge for at least an hour before serving.

BAKED BANANAS

The simplest of puddings, and an unusual one.

1 banana per person
A squeeze of lemon juice and brown sugar for serving

Put a whole, unpeeled banana in a hot oven for 7 minutes, or a medium one while you are eating your main course, and bake it until it is black. Serve the bananas hot, in their skins, but with a strip of skin peeled off the top, with a squeeze of lemon and a little brown sugar added.

CHOCOLATE BANANAS

This is another recipe from my redoubtable Scottish friend Mary and I give it here exactly as she wrote it down for me.

This is just about the quickest sweet it is possible to produce. It requires no cooking, yet is delicious and satisfying. It is easy on the purse too.

1 banana per person
4 oz. plain chocolate
Pouring cream

Cut the peeled bananas in half lengthways. Lay them in a serving dish. Grate the chocolate over them. Serve with pouring cream. One can elaborate on this if desired. For instance, some seedless raisins, soaked for 10 minutes in boiling water and then rolled in castor sugar, can be pressed into the bananas before adding the grated chocolate. A squeeze of lemon juice on the bananas gives a lovely tang.

HELEN'S FRUIT AND CHOCOLATE DIP

This is a recipe given to me by one of my Scottish friends; it is extremely quick and easy to prepare as the ingredients can be varied according to time and whatever fruit is available. Each person is given a bowl of chopped fresh fruit – either bananas, apples, grapes, oranges, etc., or a mixture of fruit – and a fork. In the middle of the table is placed a bowl of melted chocolate bar into which everyone dips their fruit. It is quite delicious. The chocolate bar, which may be Mars Bars, Toblerone or anything similar, is melted by being cut into small pieces and heated slowly in a small saucepan with 2 tablespoonfuls of water. Children love it, and it makes a lovely pudding for a casual meal with friends.

BANANA AND REDCURRANTS

In the summer, when redcurrants are cheapest, they make a delicious sharp-flavoured dessert when mixed with sliced bananas. I'm not giving proportions – use as many currants as you think you need and can afford and approximately 1 banana per person. Prepare the currants, wash them and shake off the excess liquid in a colander or sieve. Peel the bananas and cut them into rings. Mix the 2 fruits together in a bowl with enough sugar to make the currants fairly sweet and leave them to stand for as long as possible before serving, or chill in the fridge for an hour.

BANANA CUSTARD

I was a little girl during the war and didn't see a banana until I was quite big, but when it was possible to buy bananas again my mother made this pudding and I still don't know a better way of making it.

3 bananas
2 spoonfuls red jam
Juice of $\frac{1}{2}$ a lemon
1 pint of custard

Into a deep serving bowl cut the bananas into rings and squeeze over them the lemon juice. Spread the jam over the top, then pour on the custard. Serve hot or cold.

DATE CUSTARD

This is another of the puddings I remember from my childhood, eaten during the days of rationing and other horrors, and I still make it.

1 pkt. compressed dates
1 pint custard
Any left-over sponge or fruit cake (optional)

Chop the dates into little chunks. Make the custard according to the instructions on the packet and while it is still hot mix in the chopped dates really well. If you have any cake left-overs lay them in the bottom of a deep serving bowl and pour the date custard over it. Otherwise serve the custard as it is, hot or cold.

APPLE SNOW

This dessert is light and delicious for a summer evening and ideal for children, even the baby.

1 lb. cooking apples
2 tblspns. sugar (or to taste)
2 eggs
1 slice of lemon peel

Peel and core the apples and cut them into small pieces. Cook them very slowly in a covered pan with the sugar, a very little water and the little piece of lemon peel until they are pulpy. Remove the lemon peel and sieve them. Separate the eggs and mix the yolks into the cooling apples. Whip the egg whites until they are stiff but not hard and fold them into the cold apple mixture.

BAKED APPLES

4 medium-sized cooking apples
2 tblspns. golden syrup

2 oz. sultanas, raisins or chopped block dates
1 oz. butter or margarine
1 tspn. cinnamon
3 tblspns. hot water

Core the apples, but do not peel them, and place them in a fireproof dish. Cover the dried fruit with the boiling water and mix in some grated nutmeg and the cinnamon. Pack the spiced fruit into the centres of the apples, pouring over the the liquid which may be left. Pour the golden syrup over the apples, dot with the butter, cover and bake in a hot oven for about half an hour, basting them from time to time. These apples can be baked either quickly or slowly, according to whichever is more convenient at the time. They should be cooked until soft and slightly brown on the top.

APPLE DUMPLINGS

8 oz. shortcrust pastry (i.e. 8 oz. flour, 4 oz. butter
  or marge, and sufficient water to mix)
4 medium-sized cooking apples
2 oz. brown or white sugar
Nutmeg and cinnamon powder

Make the pastry in the normal way or use bought pastry. Divide it into 4 equal pieces and roll each into a circle big enough to wrap around an apple. Peel and core the apples and place each one on the centre of a pastry circle. Mix the sugar with a little nutmeg or cinnamon and pile it into the centre of each apple. Fold the pastry round the apples, moistening the edges so that the pastry will hold firmly. Place the dumplings on a baking sheet, join side down and brush them with a little milk to glaze. Bake for 30 minutes at Mark 7 (425°) until the dumplings are golden brown. The dumplings can be eaten hot or cold and may be sprinkled with a little extra white sugar when taken from the oven.

FRUIT CRUMBLE

Crumbles can be made from any stewable fruit; apples, apple and blackberry if you've been to the country for the day, rhubarb, plums, gooseberries, or, my favourite, little hard pears peeled and thinly sliced. Incidentally, any apples will do – not necessarily cooking ones. Windfalls are excellent, so are some of the really cheap little apples found in some street markets.

1½ lb. fruit
4 oz. flour
½ tspn. dried ginger
2 oz. butter or marge
2 oz. granulated sugar (or to taste)
2 oz. brown sugar or granulated
3 tblspns. water

Prepare the fruit and place it in a pie-dish with the 2 ounces of granulated sugar (or more if using sharp fruit) and the water. Sieve the flour and ginger into a mixing bowl, cut the butter into little chunks and mix it into the flour as if making pastry. When the mixture is crumbly mix in the other 2 ounces of sugar. Cover the fruit with the crumble mix and bake the pudding in a moderate oven – Mark 4 (350°) – for approximately 30 minutes, or until the top is crisp and pale golden in colour. Serve hot or cold.

STEAMED PUDDINGS

There are many variations on the theme of steamed puddings of which the most famous must be treacle or fruit pudding. I know that these puddings take a long time to cook, but the results are worth it. They are perfect for very cold days and very 'more-ish'. Here are some general instructions on how to make them; after that I just give the ingredients for each variation.

1. It is not necessary to buy packet suet; buy fresh suet cheaply from the butcher and put it through the mincer, using the fine cutter.
2. If you have any stale white bread left over use half the amount of flour and make it up to the required weight with soft breadcrumbs.
3. Always mix the suet and flour, or breadcrumbs and flour first, then add the other dry ingredients, and finally the liquid. If using eggs, mix them well before adding them to the mixture.
4. These puddings are cooked in a bowl covered with greaseproof paper or foil. The bowl and the paper or foil must be well-greased.
5. Make sure that the chosen covering, whether it's paper or foil, is closely fixed round the top of the bowl. If possible, tie a piece of string round the paper, just under the rim of the bowl.
6. The covered bowl is placed in a saucepan of boiling water to cook. The water should come half-way up the side of the bowl and should be kept topped up with boiling water so that the pudding cooks properly.
7. Fill the bowl only three-quarters full of mixture to allow room for the pudding to rise.

JAM OR MARMALADE PUDDING

**8 oz. flour or 4 oz. flour and 4 oz. soft white
  breadcrumbs
4 oz. suet
4 oz. sugar
3 tblspns. jam or marmalade
1 large egg
1 level tspn. bicarbonate of soda
Pinch of salt**

Mix the dry ingredients together. Mix the egg and bi-carbonate of soda together, mix with the jam or marmalade and add to the suet mixture. Mix everything thoroughly, turn into a geased pudding bowl and cover. Boil for 3 hours. Serve with custard or extra hot jam or marmalade.

GINGER PUDDING

8 oz. flour or 4 oz. breadcrumbs and 4 oz. flour
4 oz. suet
1 egg
3 tblspns. golden syrup
1 tspn. ground ginger
1 tblspn. milk
1 level tspn. bicarbonate of soda

Mix the dry ingredients together. Mix the bicarbonate of soda with the milk, beat the egg and add them to the dry ingredients. Finally, mix in the golden syrup and turn the mixture into a pudding bowl. Boil for 3 hours.

TREACLE PUDDING

6 oz. flour or 3 oz. flour and 3 oz. breadcrumbs
3 oz. suet
1 egg
2 tblspons. milk
1 level tspn. bicarbonate of soda
$\frac{1}{2}$ tspn. ground ginger
3 tblspns. golden syrup
$\frac{1}{2}$ tspn. salt

Mix the dry ingredients together. Beat the egg, add the bi-carbonate of soda to the milk and add them to the dry ingredients. Mix in the syrup and turn the mixture into a greased bowl. Boil for $2\frac{1}{2}$–3 hours.

DRIED FRUIT PUDDING

8 oz. flour or 4 oz. flour and 4 oz. soft white breadcrumbs
4 oz. suet
5 oz. raisins, or sultanas or currants or mixed dried fruit
1 gill milk
Pinch of salt
1 dspn. sugar
1 level tspn. bicarbonate of soda

Mix together all the dry ingredients and the fruit. Dissolve the bicarbonate of soda in the milk, add to the other in-gredients and mix thoroughly. Turn the mixture into a greased pudding bowl and boil for $2\frac{1}{2}$–3 hours.

COCONUT PUDDING

6 oz. flour or 3 oz. flour and 3 oz. breadcrumbs
3 oz. suet
4 oz. sugar
1 level tspn. bicarbonate of soda
3 oz. dessicated coconut
1 teacupful milk

Mix the dry ingredients together. Dissolve the bicarbonate of soda in the milk and mix into the other ingredients. Mix thoroughly, turn the mixture into a greased pudding bowl and boil for 2 hours.

FRUITY RICE PUDDING

1 pt. milk
2 oz. pudding rice
1 oz. raisins, or sultanas or currants
Nutmeg and cinnamon
2 oz. sugar
1 oz. butter or marge

Place the rice, sugar, fruit and the butter, cut into little pieces, in an ovenproof dish. Pour on the milk. Sprinkle over a little grated nutmeg and some cinnamon powder and bake in a low oven – Mark 2 (300°) – for about 2 hours. Rice pudding can be cooked more quickly at a higher temperature, but for the very best results it is worth letting the rice cook really slowly.

CHOCOLATE POTS

This is a very rich pudding and perfect for a supper party. Serve only small amounts in small glasses or pretty little dishes. The amounts here are for 4.

4 oz. plain chocolate
1 tblspn. cold made black coffee
3 eggs

Break the chocolate into a small pan and add the cold coffee. Over a very low heat melt the chocolate and mix it to a smooth cream. Separate the eggs and mix the yolks into the cooling chocolate. When the chocolate is cold whip the egg whites until they are stiff but not hard and fold them into the chocolate mixture. Chill for at least one hour before serving. These little puddings can be decorated with almost anything from grated chocolate to a tiny real flower stuck in the middle at the last moment, though a teaspoonful of whipped double cream is the most luxurious.

FRUIT YOGHURT

This is another almost instant pudding which is popular with everyone. For 4 people use one large carton of plain yoghurt and mix into it any chopped fresh fruit, peaches, bananas, grapes, oranges, etc., or chopped block dates and a few nuts. Serve in glasses with a sprinkling of demerara sugar on the top.

Michael Aspel

THE MEMORY BOOK
Harry Lorayne and
Jerry Lucas

You won't remember how you managed without it!

Total recall, a signpost to success, the proven method of the Lorayne School of Memory and now available to anyone interested in self-improvement. There's no magic formula, simply the basic principles of recall and practical mechanisms (the 'link' and 'peg' systems) for actual associations.

Read Lorayne's method and you will remember anything the first time you see, read or hear it.

'A never-fail system to help you remember everything *Time Magazine*

60p

STAR BOOKS

are available through all good booksellers but, where difficulty is encountered, titles can usually be obtained *by post* from:

**Star Book Service,
G.P.O. Box 29,
Douglas,
Isle of Man,
British Isles.**

Please send retail price plus 8p per copy.

Customers outside the British Isles should include 10p post/packing per copy.

Book prices are subject to alteration without notice.